DATE DUE			

THE LUCENT LIBRARY OF SCIENCE AND TECHNOLOGY

Artificial Intelligence

Other books in the Lucent Library of Science and Technology series:

Artificial Intelligence

by Peggy Thomas

LUCENT BOOKS

An imprint of Thomson Gale, a part of The Thomson Corporation

THOMSON

™

GALE

Detroit • New York • San Francisco • San Diego • New Haven, Conn. • Waterville, Maine • London • Munich

THOMSON

GALE

On cover: The robot Kismet responds with a look of wonder to re-searcher Cynthia Breazeal, who programmed it to communciate its moods through complex facial expressions.

LIBRARY OF CONGRESS CATALOGING-IN-PUBLICATION DATA

Thomas, Peggy.
 Artificial intelligence / by Peggy Thomas.
  p. cm. — (Lucent library of science and technology)
 Includes bibliographical references and index.
 ISBN 1-59018-437-8 (lib. bdg. : alk. paper)
 1. Artificial intelligence—Juvenile literature. I. Title. II. Series.
Q335.4.T48 2005
006.3—dc22   2004016477

Printed in the United States of America

Table of Contents

Foreword

"The world has changed far more in the past 100 years than in any other century in history. The reason is not political or economic, but technological—technologies that flowed directly from advances in basic science."

— Stephen Hawking, "A Brief History of Relativity," *Time,* 2000

The twentieth-century scientific and technological revolution that British physicist Stephen Hawking describes in the above quote has transformed virtually every aspect of human life at an unprecedented pace. Inventions unimaginable a century ago have not only become commonplace but are now considered necessities of daily life. As science historian James Burke writes, "We live surrounded by objects and systems that we take for granted, but which profoundly affect the way we behave, think, work, play, and in general conduct our lives."

For example, in just one hundred years, transportation systems have dramatically changed. In 1900 the first gasoline-powered motorcar had just been introduced, and only 144 miles of U.S. roads were hard-surfaced. Horse-drawn trolleys still filled the streets of American cities. The airplane had yet to be invented. Today 217 million vehicles speed along 4 million miles of U.S. roads. Humans have flown to the moon and commercial aircraft are capable of transporting passengers across the Atlantic Ocean in less than three hours.

The transformation of communications has been just as dramatic. In 1900 most Americans lived and worked on farms without electricity or mail delivery. Few people had ever heard a radio or spoken on a telephone. A hundred years later, 98 percent of American homes have telephones and televisions and more than 50 percent have personal computers. Some families even have more than one television and computer, and cell phones are now commonplace, even among the young. Data beamed from communication satellites routinely predict global weather conditions, and fiber-optic cable, e-mail, and the Internet have made worldwide telecommunication instantaneous.

Perhaps the most striking measure of scientific and technological change can be seen in medicine and public health. At the beginning of the twentieth century, the average American life span was forty-seven years. By the end of the century the average life span was approaching eighty years, thanks to advances in medicine including the development of vaccines and antibiotics, the discovery of powerful diagnostic tools such as X-rays, the life-saving technology of cardiac and neonatal care, and improvements in nutrition and the control of infectious disease.

Rapid change is likely to continue throughout the twenty-first century as science reveals more about physical and biological processes such as global warming, viral replication, and electrical conductivity, and as people apply that new knowledge to personal decisions and government policy. Already, for example, an international treaty calls for immediate reductions in industrial and automobile emissions in response to studies that show a potentially dangerous rise in global temperatures is caused by human activity. Taking an active role in determining the direction of future changes depends on education; people must understand the possible uses of scientific research and the effects of the technology that surrounds them.

The Lucent Books Library of Science and Technology profiles key innovations and discoveries that have transformed the modern world. Each title strives to make a complex scientific discovery, technology, or phenomenon understandable and relevant to the reader. Because scientific discovery is rarely straightforward, each title explains the dead ends, fortunate accidents, and basic scientific methods by which the research into the subject proceeded. And every book examines the practical applications of an invention, branch of science, or scientific principle in industry, public health, and personal life, as well as potential future uses and effects based on ongoing research. Fully documented quotations, annotated bibliographies that include both print and electronic sources, glossaries, indexes, and technical illustrations are among the supplemental features designed to point researchers to further exploration of the subject.

Introduction

Fact Follows Fiction

As far back as the ancient Greek civilization, people have imagined machines and mechanical men that could work and think like any human. One Greek myth, for example, tells of the Greek god Hephaestus, who built mechanical men to forge powerful weapons and spectacular jewelry. When the king of Crete requested that he make a giant man to guard his island, Hephaestus constructed the metallic warrior Talos. Talos patrolled the shores of Crete until Jason and the Argonauts defeated it.

In the late 1800s, as the genre of science fiction developed, books about intelligent machines serving human masters sparked the public's imagination, but not until the 1920s did such machines acquire the name *robot*. In 1920 Czech playwright Karel Capek published the play *R.U.R. (Rossum's Universal Robots)* in which the character Professor Rossum manufactures artificial men to do all the menial chores, called *robota* in the Czech language. Rossum's plan backfires and armies of robots are purchased by warring nations. Eventually the robots themselves revolt and attempt to take over all of humankind.

In the 1950s and 1960s a series of movies and books portrayed the blessings but more often the horrors of intelligent machines, which took all forms. Some were Talos-like robots made of shiny metal, like Gort in *The*

Day the Earth Stood Still (1951); others were intelligent supercomputers that threatened to take over the world in movies like *Colossus: The Forbin Project* (1969). In this film the supercomputer that ran the U.S. national defense systems overrode all human control. But perhaps the most famous malevolent supercomputer was HAL 9000, the sinister manager of the spaceship *Discovery* in *2001: A Space Odyssey* (1968). HAL could learn and act independent of human input and in so doing it killed all but one crew member.

Filmmaker George Lucas created the lovable robots R2-D2 and C-3PO for his popular science fiction saga Star Wars.

Not all robots or supercomputers have been portrayed as evil. In the 1970s moviegoers fell in love with the flighty C-3PO and quirky trashcan-shaped R2-D2 in the *Star Wars* series. Without the help of these autonomous beings, the heroes would not have prevailed over the evil empire. And in 2001 audiences connected with the boy robot in Steven Spielberg's film *AI* when he expresses emotions and feelings of love toward his adoptive human parents.

These fictional stories reflect humans' dreams and fears about intelligent machines. And there is an odd correlation between science fiction and science fact. Writers have envisioned worlds that are technologically several steps ahead of reality. They imagined robots on Mars long before the first moon landing and portable minicomputers long before the invention of laptops.

Scientists who work in the field of artificial intelligence (AI), the study of intelligent machines, also foresee a future filled with independent, thinking robots and computer companions. Unlike fiction writers, however, they face the daunting challenge of making their dreams a reality. Each year AI researchers come closer to realizing their dreams with new developments in computer programming and robotic engineering.

Real-life AI

As in fictional stories, the pursuit of intelligent machines has taken two forms. Researchers have created robotic bodies—like that of C-3PO—that look and move like a human. They have even created artificial material similar to human skin that will mask the computer chips and wiring inside a robot's head. Other researchers are working on robots that learn from experience—like those in Isaac Asimov's classic story *I, Robot*—and can express emotions like the robotic boy in director Steven Spielberg's feature film *AI*.

The second form of intelligent machines is the all-knowing and all-powerful "beings without bodies" like HAL. Artificial intelligence experts have already created supercomputers that navigate and control the space shuttles; other computer systems are powerful enough to effectively run major companies. But AI is not just reserved for grand space exploration or high finance. In fact, much of a person's daily life is affected by some form of artificial intelligence. AI computer programs keep track of a person's banking, translate foreign languages, locate a car's position, and put once hard-to-find information at a person's fingertips with the Internet. Each year smart machines become more proficient at chores we used to do for ourselves, and people purchase the newest electronic AI gadgets in hopes of making their lives easier. But what happens to a society that gives more and more control to machines? Will fact follow fiction? Will people enjoy a life of friendly companionship with robots like R2-D2 and live blissfully by relying on all-knowing machines to help them get through their days?

Anyone who has been beaten by a computer at a game of chess knows the unsettling feeling of dealing with an intelligent system. Will that unease grow? And as more jobs are given to computers, how will that change humanity? Will people lose skills like remembering phone numbers or calculating large sums? Will people become slaves to the very machines they have created and lose their humanity in a world of mechanization? Will the fictional cautionary tales be heeded, or will the future hold a wondrous collaboration between man and machine? Only time will tell as scientists continue to forge ahead and attempt to make real the amazing dreams of fiction writers.

Chapter 1

The First Thinking Machines

G aak was missing. No one knew what it was thinking or if it was thinking at all. The only thing that robotics expert Noel Sharkey knew was that the small robotic unit he had just repaired had disappeared. Gaak had been injured in battle during a "survival of the fittest" demonstration at the Living Robots exhibition in Rotherham, England, in 2002. In this contest predator robots sought out prey robots to drain their energy, and prey robots had to learn to avoid capture or be inactivated.

Gaak, a predator robot, may have had enough of the competition. Only fifteen minutes after Sharkey left the robot's side, the autonomous machine forced its way out of its corral, sidled past hundreds of spectators, maneuvered down an exit ramp, and left the building. Gaak's bid for freedom was stopped short when it was almost run over by a car as it fled toward the exit gate.

Although this may sound like another sci-fi nightmare, it is actually an example of artificial intelligence at work today. AI is the study and creation of machines that can perform tasks that would require intelligence if a human were to do the same job. This emerging and constantly changing field combines computer programming, robotics engineering, mathematics, neurology, and even psychology. As a blend of many sciences, AI has a scattered history. It has almost as many processes as there are researchers active in the field. Like the limbs of a tree, each new idea spawns another, and the science of artificial intelligence has many branches. But its roots were planted by scientists and mathematicians who could imagine all the possibilities and who created amazing machines that startled the world.

The Analytical Engine

The first glimmer of a "thinking machine" came in the 1830s when British mathematician Charles Babbage envisioned what he called the analytical engine. Babbage was a highly regarded professor of mathematics at Cambridge University when he resigned his position to devote all of his energies to his revolutionary idea.

In the 1830s, British mathematician Charles Babbage envisioned the world's first intelligent machines.

In Babbage's time, the complex mathematical tables used by ship's captains to navigate the seas, as well as many other intricate computations, had to be calculated by teams of mathematicians who were called computers. No matter how painstaking these human computers were, their tables were often full of errors. Babbage wanted to create a machine that could automatically calculate a mathematical chart or table in much less time and with more accuracy. His mechanical computer, designed with cogs and gears and powered by steam, was capable of performing multiple tasks by simple reprogramming—or changing the instructions given to the computer.

The idea of one machine performing many tasks was inspired by the giant industrial Jacquard looms built by French engineer Joseph-Marie Jacquard in 1805. These looms performed mechanical actions in response to cards that had holes punched in them. Each card provided

Babbage's Difference Engine

Although no one may ever see a real example of Charles Babbage's ingenious Analytical Engine, a Difference Engine was re-created in the 1990s from Babbage's original drawings by a team of engineers at London's Science Museum. Made of cast iron, bronze, and steel, the workable machine stands ten feet wide and six feet high and weighs three tons. The Difference Engine performs mathematical computations that are accurate up to thirty-one digits. But unlike the Analytical Engine, Babbage's Difference Engine is powered by hand. The computer operator has to turn a crank hundreds of times to perform one calculation.

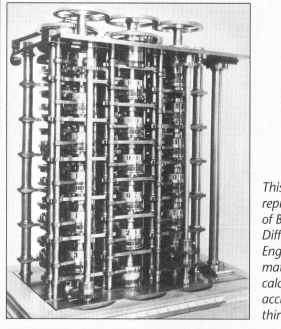

This recent reproduction of Babbage's Difference Engine performs mathematical calculations accurate to thirty-one digits.

the pattern that the loom would follow; different cards would instruct the loom to weave different patterns. Babbage realized that the instructions fed into a machine could just as easily represent the sequence of instructions needed to perform a mathematical calculation as it could a weaving pattern.

His first attempt was called the Difference Engine. It could translate instructions punched on input cards into arrangements of mechanical parts, store variables in specially positioned wheels, perform the logical operations with gears, and deliver the results on punched output cards. Only one small version of the Difference Engine was created before Babbage turned his attention to a more ambitious machine that could perform more abstract "thinking."

Babbage's second design was a larger machine called the Analytical Engine. It was designed to perform many different kinds of computations such as those needed to create navigational tables and read symbols other than numbers. His partner in this venture was Lady Ada Lovelace, daughter of the poet Lord Byron. Unlike her father, who had a talent for words, the countess had a head for numbers. She is often credited with inventing computer programming, the process of writing instructions that tell a computer or machine what to do. Of Babbage's machine she said, "The Analytical Engine weaves algebraical patterns just as the Jacquard Loom weaves flowers and leaves."[1]

Unfortunately Lovelace was never able to program one of Babbage's machines. As a result of financial problems and the difficulty of manufacturing precision parts for his machine, Babbage had to abandon his project. Almost a century and a half would pass before a similar machine was assembled. Seldom has such a long time separated an idea and its technological application.

The Turing Machine

The next and perhaps most influential machine to mark the development of AI was, once again, never even built. It was a theoretical machine, an idea that existed only on paper. Devised by the brilliant British theoretical mathematician Alan Turing in 1936, this simple machine consisted of a program, a data storage device (or memory), and a step-by-step method of computation. The mechanism would pass a long thin tape of paper, like that in a ticker-tape machine, through a processing head that would read the information. This apparatus would be able to move the paper along, read a series of symbols, and produce calculations based on the input on the tape. The so-called universal computer, or Turing machine, became the ideal model for scores of other researchers who eventually developed the modern digital computer. Less than ten years later, the three most powerful nations in the world had working computers that played an integral part in World War II.

The Giants of the Computer Age

Teams of British mathematicians, logicians, and engineers created a computer called Colossus, which was used to decode secret enemy messages intercepted from Germany. The advantage of Colossus was that

Dr. J.W. Mauchly makes an adjustment to ENIAC, the massive computer he designed to assist the U.S. military during World War II.

the British military did not have to wait days for a team of human decoders to unravel secret plans. Colossus could decode messages within hours. It helped save lives and was a key factor in the Allied forces' defeat of the Germans.

In the meantime, German mathematicians and computer programmers had created a computer to rival Colossus. Called Z3, the German computer was used to design military aircraft. The United States also entered the computer age with the development of a computer called the Electronic Numerical Integrator and Computer, or ENIAC, which churned out accurate ballistic charts that showed the trajectory of bombs for the U.S. Navy.

ENIAC, Z3, and Colossus were monsters compared to modern-day computers. ENIAC weighed in at thirty tons, took up three rooms, and consisted of seventeen thousand vacuum tubes that controlled the flow of electricity. However, these tubes tended to pop, flare up, and die out like fireworks on the Fourth of July. Six full-time technicians had to race around to replace bulbs and literally debug the system: Hundreds of moths, attracted to the warm glow of the vacuum tubes, would get inside the machine and gum up the circuits.

The Binary Code

ENIAC and all other computers that have followed have spoken the same basic language: the binary code. This is a system of symbols used to program a computer. Proposed by U.S. mathematician Claude Shannon and expanded on by Hungarian-born mathematician John von Neumann in the 1940s, the binary code is a language with only two symbols, 0 and 1. Shannon and von Neumann showed that the simplest instruction was yes/no, or the flicking on and off of a switch, and that any logical task could be broken down to this switching network of two symbols. The system is binary, based on two digits, and combinations of these two digits, or bits, represent all other numbers.

Binary Code

Computers use a binary number system to quickly process information. Electrical pulses travel through millions of transistors, which are miniature electric switches that have two positions: on and off. When a switch is on, it represents binary digit 1. When a switch is off, it represents binary digit 0.

The English alphabet in binary code:

A	01000001	G	01000111	M	01001101	S	01010011	Y	01011001
B	01000010	H	01001000	N	01001110	T	01010100	Z	01011010
C	01000011	I	01001001	O	01001111	U	01010101		
D	01000100	J	01001010	P	01010000	V	01010110		
E	01000101	K	01001011	Q	01010001	W	01010111		
F	01000110	L	01001100	R	01010010	X	01011000		

The words _ARTIFICIAL INTELLIGENCE_ look like this in binary code:

01000001 01010010 01010100 01001001 01000110 01001001 01000011 01001001

01000001 01001100 00100000 01001001 01001110 01010100 01000101 01001100

01001100 01001001 01000111 01000101 01001110 01000011 01000101

Inside the computer, electrical circuits operate as switches. When a switch is on, it represents the binary digit 1. When a switch is off, it represents the binary digit 0. This type of calculation is fast and can be manipulated to count, add, subtract, multiply, divide, compare, list, or rearrange according to the program. This simple digital system can be used to program a computer to do even the most complex tasks. The results of electrical circuits manipulating strings of binary digits are then translated into letters or numbers that people can understand. For instance, the letter A is represented by the binary number 01000001. Today, by reading and changing binary digits, a machine can display a Shakespearean sonnet, play a Mozart melody, run a blockbuster movie, and even represent the entire sequence of human DNA.

Smaller and Faster

The basic digital language of early computers was fast, but the hardware that performed the tasks was not. Vacuum tubes were unreliable and broke down frequently. Computing was made faster with transistors, a crucial invention developed in the 1950s. A transistor is a miniature electronic switch that has two operating positions: on and off. It is the basic building block of a computer that enables it to process information. Transistors are made from silicon, a type of material that is called a semiconductor because certain impurities introduced to the silicon affect how an electrical current flows through it.

These early transistors were lighter, more durable, and longer lasting. They required less energy and did not attract moths, as ENIAC's vacuum tubes did. They were also smaller, about the size of a man's thumb. And smaller translated to faster. The shorter the distance the electronic signal traveled, the faster the calculation.

The next improvement came with the invention of the integrated circuit, an arrangement of tiny transistors on a sliver, or chip, of silicon that dramatically reduced the distance traveled. The amount of infor-

A Science Gets a Name

In pursuit of a machine that could pass the Turing Test, a group of researchers held a conference in 1956. Called the Dartmouth Conference, it was an open invitation to all researchers studying or trying to apply intelligence to a machine. This conference became famous not necessarily because of those who attended (although some of the most well-known AI experts were there) but because of the ideas that were presented. At the conference the researchers put forth a mission statement about their work. Quoted in Daniel Crevier's 1993 book *AI: The Tumultuous History of the Search for Artificial Intelligence,* the mission statement said, "Every aspect of learning or any other feature of intelligence can in principle be so precisely described that a machine can be made to simulate it." And the researchers came up with a name for their pursuits that became accepted worldwide and solidified a science—artificial intelligence.

mation held in a given amount of space also increased drastically. A vacuum tube, for example, could fit one bit of information in a space the size of a thumb. One of the first transistors could hold one bit in a space the size of a fingernail. Today a modern silicon microchip the size of a grain of rice can contain millions of bits of information. These rapid improvements in computing technology allowed for rapid advancements in the pursuit of artificial intelligence.

The Turing Test

In 1950 Alan Turing solidified his place as the grandfather of AI with his paper "Computing Machinery and Intelligence." The now-famous report claimed that computing technology would one day improve to the point where machines would be considered intelligent. He knew this claim would be difficult to prove, so he also put forth the idea of a standardized test he called the Imitation Game. Now known as the Turing Test, it is set up in the following manner: An interrogator or judge sits in front of two computer terminals. One terminal is connected to a person in another room; the other terminal to a computer in a third room. The interrogator types questions on both terminals to try to figure out which terminal is controlled by a human and which is controlled by a machine. If the interrogator cannot decide which contestant is human, or chooses incorrectly, then the computer would be judged intelligent.

Turing's paper and theoretical test was another milestone in the development of AI. He predicted that by the year 2000 a computer "would be able to play the imitation game so well that an average interrogator will not have more than a 70 percent chance of making the right identification (machine or human) after five minutes of questioning."[2]

The year 2000 has come and gone and no machine has yet passed the test. But the lack of a winner has not deterred AI programmers in their quest. Today an annual contest called the Loebner Prize offers $100,000 to the creator of the first machine to pass the Turing Test.

Some people argue that the Turing Test must be flawed. With all that artificial intelligence can do, it seems illogical to them that a machine cannot pass the test. But the importance of the Turing Test is that it gives researchers a clear goal in their quest for a thinking machine. Turing himself suggested that the game of chess would be a good avenue to explore in the search for intelligent machines, and that pursuit led to the development of another machine that made early AI history.

Deep Blue

The complex game of chess involves intellectual strategy and an almost endless array of moves. According to one calculation there are 10^{120} (or 10 followed by 120 zeros) possible moves. In comparison, the entire universe is believed to contain only 10^{75} atoms. Of course, no player could consider all possible moves, but the best players are capable of thinking ahead, anticipating their opponent's play, and instantaneously selecting small subsets of best moves from which to choose in response. Prompted by Turing's suggestion that chess was a good indicator of intelligence, many AI groups around the world began to develop a chess-playing computer. The first tournament match that pitted a computer against a human occurred in 1967. But it was not until the 1980s that computers became good enough to defeat an experienced player. A computer called Deep Thought, created by students at Carnegie Mellon University in Pittsburgh, beat grand master Brent Larsen at a single game in 1988.

A team from IBM took over Deep Thought, reconfigured its programming, dressed it in blue, and renamed the new chess-playing computer Deep Blue. Deep Blue's strength was sheer power: It was so fast it could evaluate 200 million positions per second and

look fifteen to thirty moves ahead. Its human opponent, the world chess champion Gary Kasparov of Russia, could consider only three moves per second. Deep Blue, outweighing its human opponent by almost a ton, won its first game in 1996. Kasparov fought back and managed to win the match four games to two. A rematch held on May 10, 1997, again pitted a souped-up Deep Blue against Kasparov. Deep Blue won every game in the match. In an interview afterward, Kasparov admitted that he "sensed a new kind of intelligence"[3] fighting against him.

Chess champion Gary Kasparov executes a move during a 1997 match against the highly sophisticated computer Deep Blue as the computer's designer watches.

Shakey the Robot

While some researchers were making headlines playing computer chess, others were exploring the combination of robotics and AI. In 1969 Nils Nilsson at Stanford University created an early AI robot called Shakey. This five-foot-tall boxy robot earned its nickname from the video camera and TV transmitter mast

extending from its top, which shook back and forth
as the robot moved. Shakey's world was limited to a
set of carefully constructed rooms. It was programmed
with an internal map of the dimension and position
of every object in the rooms so that it would not bump
into anything. Shakey moved around at the snail-like
speed of one foot every five minutes, stopping peri-
odically to "see" its environment through the camera
lens, which transmitted images to the computer. It

*Computer scientist
Charles Rosen poses
next to Shakey, an
early AI robot that
was able to move
about without
bumping into objects.*

would then "think" of its next move. If someone came in and moved objects in the room while Shakey was "thinking," the robot would not notice and inevitably bump into the moved objects.

Shakey's program was so immense that it could not carry the necessary computer power around with it. It had to be attached by a thick cable to its electronic brain, located in another room. Because of its tethered existence and programmed environment, Shakey could not function outside of its own little world. But its importance lay in what it taught AI researchers about intelligence and the real world.

Machines like Deep Blue and Shakey represent the traditional era of AI. Traditional AI specialists thought —and some still do think—that human intelligence is based on symbols that can be manipulated and processed. Intelligence was equated with knowledge. The more facts people or computers knew, the more intelligent they were. That is why early AI projects focused on things that most people, including college professors, found challenging, like playing chess, proving mathematical theorems, and solving complicated algebraic problems.

Early AI researchers believed that the human brain worked like a computer, taking in information and converting it to symbols, which were processed by the brain and then converted back to a recognizable form as a thought. Every aspect of Shakey's world was programmed using the digital binary code so that the machine could perceive changes and operate within its mapped world. Deep Blue's chess program was created the same way. This traditional AI, although very rigid, had amazing success. It was the basis of programs called expert systems, the first form of AI put to practical, commercial use.

Expert Systems

An expert system is an AI program that imitates the knowledge and decision-making abilities of a person with expertise in a certain field. These programs provide a second opinion and are designed to help people make sound decisions. An expert system has two parts—a knowledge base and an inference engine.

The knowledge base is created by knowledge engineers, who interview dozens of human experts in the field. For example, if an expert system is intended to help doctors diagnose patients' illnesses, then knowledge engineers would interview many doctors about their process of diagnosing illnesses. What symptoms do they look for, and what assumptions do they make? These questions are not easy to answer, because a person's knowledge depends on something more than facts. Often experts use words like *intuition* or *hunch* to express what they know. Underlying that hunch, however, are dozens of tiny, subconscious facts or rules of thumb that an expert or doctor has already learned. When those rules of thumb are programmed into a computer, the result is an expert system. "Real [stock market] analysts think what they do is some sort of art, but it can really be reduced to rules,"[4] says Edgar Peters of PanAgora Asset Management. This is true for most decision-making procedures.

The second part of an expert system, the inference engine, is a logic program that interprets the instructions and evaluates the facts to make a decision. It operates on an if-then type of logic program—for example, "if the sun is shining, then it must be daytime." Every inference engine contains thousands of these if-then instructions.

The first expert systems were used in medicine, business, and finance to help doctors and business managers make better decisions. Expert systems are still used today in the stock market, banking, and military defense.

Intelligence or Imitation?

Traditional AI represents only one type of intelligence. It is very effective at applying knowledge to a single problem, but over time, it became apparent that traditional expert systems were too limited and specialized. A chess program like Deep Blue could play one of the most difficult strategy games in the world, but it could not play checkers or subtract two-digit numbers, and it performed its operations without any understanding of what it was doing.

In 1980 John Searle, a U.S. philosopher, described artificial intelligence with an analogy he called the Chinese room. Suppose an English-speaking person is sitting in a closed room with only a giant rule book of the Chinese language to keep him company. The book enables the person to look up Chinese sentences and offers sentences to be used in reply. The person receives written messages through a hole in the wall. Using the rule book, he looks up the sentences, responds to them, and slips the response back through the hole in the wall. From outside the room it appears that the person inside is fluent in the Chinese language, when in reality, the person is only carrying out a simple operation of matching symbols on a page without any understanding of the messages coming in or going out of the hole.

Searle's analogy made researchers wonder. Was AI just an imitation of human intelligence? Was intelligence simply the processing of information and spitting out of answers, or was there more to it than that?

Chapter 2

Mind Versus Metal

The activities that kindergarten-age children perform effortlessly, like knowing the difference between a cup and a chair, or walking from one room to the next without bumping into the wall, were not thought of as intelligent behavior or worthy of study by traditional AI researchers. But when traditional systems did not perform as they had expected, experts in AI began to wonder what intelligence really meant. They also began to think about different ways to show intelligence in a machine. Although the definition of intelligence is still debated today, scientists understand that intelligence is more than the sum of facts a person knows; it also derives from what a person experiences and how a person perceives the world around him or her. Neil Gershenfeld, author of *When Things Start to Think*, believes that "we need all of our senses to make sense of the world, and so do computers."[5] As ideas about human intelligence changed, so did approaches to creating artificial intelligence.

In the 1980s AI experts working in robotics began to realize that the simple activities humans take for granted are much more difficult to replicate in a machine than anyone thought. As expert AI researcher Stewart Wilson of the Roland Institute in Cambridge explains:

> AI projects were masterpieces of programming that dealt with various fragments of human intelligence. . . . But they were too specialized. . . . They couldn't take raw input from the world

around them; they had to sit there waiting for a human to hand them symbols, and they then manipulated the symbols without knowing what they meant. None of these programs could learn from or adapt to the world around them. Even the simplest animals can do these things, but they had been completely ignored by AI.[6]

Breaking away from traditional AI programming, some researchers veered off to study the lower-level intelligence displayed by animals. One such person is Rodney Brooks, the director of the Computer Science and Artificial Intelligence Laboratory at the Massachusetts Institute of Technology (MIT).

Insect Intelligence

Brooks started at the bottom of the evolutionary ladder, with insects, which were already capable of doing what the most sophisticated AI machines could not do. Insects can move at speeds of a meter or more per second, avoid obstacles in their path, evade predators, and seek out mates and food without having to

The six-legged insectlike robot known as Genghis is programmed to home in on objects by tracking the heat they give off.

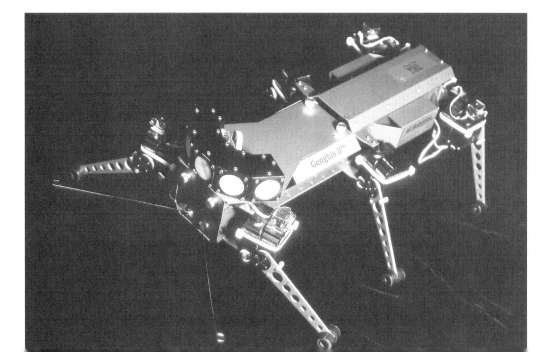

have a mental map as Shakey the robot did. Instead of preprogramming behaviors, Brooks programmed in less information, just enough to enable his AI robots to adapt to objects in their path. He felt that navigation and perception were key to mastering higher-level intelligence. This trend became known as the bottom-up approach, in contrast to the top-down approach of programming in all necessary information.

Brooks's focus was creating a machine that could perceive the world around it and react to it. As a result, he created Genghis, a six-legged insectlike robot. According to Brooks, "When powered off, it sat on the floor with its legs sprawled out flat. When it was switched on, it would stand up and wait to see some moving infrared source. As soon as its beady array of six sensors caught sight of something, it was off."[7] Its six sensors picked up on the heat of a living creature, such as a person or a dog, and triggered the stalking mode. It would scramble to its feet and follow its prey, moving around furniture and climbing over obstacles to keep the prey in sight.

Brooks's machine could "see" and adapt to its environment, but it could not perform higher-level intelligent behaviors at the same time. A man, for example, can make a mental grocery list while he is walking down the street to the store; a woman can carry on a conversation with a passenger while driving safely down the road and looking for an address. Researchers began to ask, how is the human brain able to perform so many tasks at the same time?

How the Brain Works

The human brain has close to 100 billion nerve cells, called neurons. Each neuron is connected to thousands of others, creating a neural network that shuttles information in the form of stimuli, in and out of the brain constantly.

Each neuron is made up of four main parts: the synapses, soma, axon, and dendrites. The soma is the

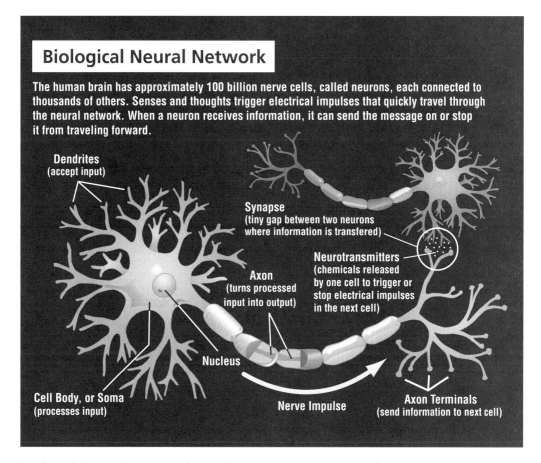

Biological Neural Network

The human brain has approximately 100 billion nerve cells, called neurons, each connected to thousands of others. Senses and thoughts trigger electrical impulses that quickly travel through the neural network. When a neuron receives information, it can send the message on or stop it from traveling forward.

Dendrites
(accept input)

Synapse
(tiny gap between two neurons
where information is transfered)

Neurotransmitters
(chemicals released
by one cell to trigger or
stop electrical impulses
in the next cell)

Axon
(turns processed
input into output)

Nucleus

Cell Body, or Soma
(processes input)

Nerve Impulse

Axon Terminals
(send information to next cell)

body of the cell where the information is processed. Each neuron has long, thin nerve fibers called dendrites that bring information in and even longer fibers called axons that send information away. The neuron receives information in the form of electrical signals from neighboring neurons across one of thousands of synapses, small gaps that separate two neurons and act as input channels.

Once a neuron has received this charge it triggers either a "go" signal that allows the message to be passed to the next neuron or a "stop" signal that prevents the message from being forwarded. When a person thinks of something, sees an image, or smells a scent, that mental process or sensory stimulus excites a neuron, which fires an electrical pulse that shoots out through the axons and fires across the synapse. If enough input is received at the same time, the neuron is activated to send out a signal to be picked up by the next neuron's dendrites. Most of the brain consists of the "wiring" between the neurons, which makes up one thousand trillion connections. If these fibers were real wire, they would measure out to an estimated 63,140 miles inside the average skull.

Each stimulus leads to a chain reaction of electrical impulses, and the brain is constantly firing and rewiring itself. When neurons repeatedly fire in a particular pattern, that pattern becomes a semipermanent feature of the brain. Learning comes when patterns are strengthened, but if connections are not stimulated, they are weakened. For example, the more a student repeats the number to open a combination lock, the more the connections that take in that information are bolstered to create a stronger memory that will be easily retrieved the next time. At the end of the school year, when a student puts the lock away, that number will not be used for a couple of months. Those three numbers will be much harder to recall when fall comes and that student needs to open the lock again.

Artificial Neural Networks

The branch of AI that modeled its work after the neural network of the human brain is called connectionism. It is based on the belief that the way the brain works is all about making the right connections, and those connections can just as easily be made using silicon and wire as living neurons and dendrites.

Called artificial neural networks (ANNs), these programs work in the same way as the brain's neural network. An artificial neuron has a number of connections or inputs. To mimic a real neuron, each input is weighted with a fraction between 0 and 1. The weight indicates how important the incoming signal for that input is going to be. An input weighted 0.4 is more important than an input weighted 0.1. All of the incoming signals' weights are added together and the total sum equals the net value of the neuron.

Each artificial neuron is also given a number that represents the threshold or point over which the artificial neuron will fire and send on the signal to another neuron. If the net value is greater than the threshold, the neuron will fire. If the value is less than the threshold, it will not fire. The output from the firing is then passed on to other neurons that are weighted as well. For example, the computer's goal is to answer the question, Will the teacher give a quiz on Friday? To help answer the question, the programmer provides these weighted inputs:

The teacher loves giving quizzes = 0.2.

The teacher has not given a quiz in two weeks = 0.1.

The teacher gave the last three quizzes on Fridays = 0.3.

The sum of the input weights equals 0.6. The threshold assigned to that neuron is 0.5. In this case, the net value of the neuron exceeds the threshold number so the artificial neuron is fired. This process occurs again and again in rapid succession until the process is completed.

If the ANN is wrong, and the teacher does not give a quiz on Friday, then the weights are lowered. Each time a correct connection is made, the weight is increased. The next time the question is asked, the ANN will be more likely to answer correctly. The proper connections are weighted so that there is more chance that the machine will choose that connection the next time. After hundreds of repeated training processes, the correct neural network connections are strengthened and remembered, just like a memory in the human brain. This is how the ANN is trained rather than programmed with specific information. A well-trained ANN is said to be able to learn. In this way the computer is learning much like a child learns, through trial and error. Unlike a child, however, a computer can make millions of trial-and-error attempts at lightning speed.

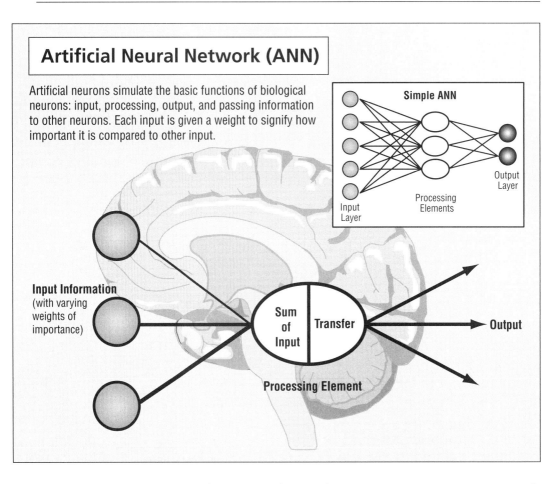

Artificial Neural Network (ANN)

Artificial neurons simulate the basic functions of biological neurons: input, processing, output, and passing information to other neurons. Each input is given a weight to signify how important it is compared to other input.

Simple ANN

Input Layer

Processing Elements

Output Layer

Input Information (with varying weights of importance)

Sum of Input

Transfer

Output

Processing Element

Whereas traditional AI expert systems are specialized and inflexible, ANN systems are trainable and more flexible, and they can deal with a wide range of data and information. They can also learn from their mistakes. This kind of AI is best for analyzing and recognizing patterns.

Pattern Recognition

Pattern recognition may seem obvious or trivial, but it is an essential, basic component of the way people learn. Looking around a room, a child learns the patterns of the room's layout and recognizes objects in the room. People know that a pencil is a pencil because of the pattern the pencil presents to them. They

learn and become familiar with that pattern. Learning
a language is actually the activity of learning numerous patterns in letters, syllables, and sentences.
The first ANN prototype, Perceptron, created in the
1950s, was trained to perform the difficult task of
identifying and recognizing the letters of the alphabet. Today more sophisticated ANNs are also capable
of finding patterns in auditory data. ANN software or
programs are used to analyze handwriting, compare
fingerprints, process written and oral language, and
translate languages.

Incorporated into expert systems, ANNs can provide a more flexible program that can learn new patterns as time goes on. They are especially useful when
all the facts are not known. These programs have
proven more reliable than humans when analyzing
applications for credit cards or home mortgage loans.
An ANN system can find patterns in data that are un-
detectable to the human eye. Such tracking is called
data mining, and oftentimes the outcome is surprising. For example, the sophisticated computers that
keep track of Wal-Mart's sales discovered an odd relationship between the sale of diapers and the sale of
beer. It appeared that on Friday nights the sales of both
products increased.

Some police departments use an ANN search engine
called Coplink to search multiple case files from different locations and criminal databases to find patterns to seemingly unrelated crimes. Coplink helped
catch the two snipers convicted of a string of shoot-
ings in the Washington, D.C., area in 2002.

The Chicago police department uses another ANN
program called Brainmaker to predict which police of-
ficers would be more likely to become corrupt and not
perform their job according to the oath they took upon
becoming an officer. Another software product called
True Face recognizes human faces by comparing video
images to thousands of stored images in its memory
in spite of wigs, glasses, makeup, or bad lighting.

Breeding Programs

Another model of machine learning is based on the biological system of genetics, in which systems change over time. Introduced by John Henry Holland at MIT in the 1950s, this kind of system uses genetic algorithms. An algorithm is simply a step-by-step process of solving a specific problem. An algorithm comes in many forms, but usually it is a set of rules by which a process is run. In a genetic system an algorithm is made up of an array of bits or characters, much like a chromosome is made up of bits of DNA. Each bit is encoded with certain variables of the problem or with functions used in solving the problem. Just as a gene would carry specific information about the makeup of an organism (blue or green eyes), a bit might select for functions of addition or subtraction.

In traditional AI, algorithms would be programmed into a system to perform the same task over and over again without variation. But in a genetic system the computer is given a large pool of chromosomes or bit

A Commonsense Computer

According to expert Marvin Minsky, as quoted in the *Overview of Cycorp's Research and Development*, the one problem with artificial intelligence is that "people have silly reasons why computers don't really think. The answer is we haven't programmed them right; they just don't have common sense." Common sense allows a person to make assumptions, jump to conclusions, and make sound decisions based on common knowledge.

Doug Lenat took up the challenge and created Cyc, a program named after the word *encyclopedia*. For more than twenty years, Lenat and his team at Cycorp has fed the Cyc system with every bit of knowledge that a typical adult would or should know; for example, that George Washington was the first president, that plants perform photosynthesis, that it snows in Minnesota, that e-mail is an Internet communication, and that beavers build dams. The idea behind this long-term project is that Cyc will be able to make reasonable assumptions with the knowledge it has been given. For example, if a person said that he or she had read Melville, Cyc might assume that the person had read the author Herman Melville's most famous book, *Moby Dick*.

strings encoded with various bits of information. The bit strings are tested to see how well they perform at the task at hand. The algorithms that perform the best are then bred using the genetic concepts of mutation and crossover to create a new generation of algorithms. Mutations occur by randomly flipping the location of bits on the chromosome. Mutations can bring about drastic random change that may or may not improve the next generation. Crossover occurs when two parent programs trade and insert fragments from one to the other. This ensures that groups of bits or genes that work well together stay together.

With each change, the procedure creates new combinations. Some may work better than the parent generation and others may not. Those algorithms that do not perform well are dropped out of the system like a weak fledgling from a nest. Those that perform better become part of the breeding process. Genetic programs can be run many times, creating thousands of generations in a day. Each time bits of information are changed and the set of rules are improved until an adequate solution to the problem is found.

The kinds of problems that genetic algorithms are most useful at solving involve a large number of possible solutions. They are fondly called traveling salesman problems, after the classic example of a salesperson finding the shortest route to take to visit a set number of towns. With five towns to visit, there are 120 possible routes to take, but with twenty-five towns to visit, there are 155×10^{23} (or 155 followed by 23 zeros) possible routes and finding the shortest route becomes an almost insurmountable task.

Such a task is a common one in real life. It is a problem for airlines that need to schedule the arrivals and departures of hundreds of planes and for manufacturers who need to figure out the most efficient order in which to assemble their product. Phone companies also need to figure out the best way to organize their network so that every call gets through quickly.

Genetic algorithms are also used to program the way a robot moves. There are an almost infinite number of potential moves, and genetic algorithms find the most efficient method. After all of the genetic algorithms have evolved, the genetic program produces an overall strategy using the best moves for certain situations. The best performing programs are then taken out of the robots and reassembled to produce a new generation of mobile robots.

In the future, these genetic systems may even evolve into software that can write itself. Two parent programs will combine to create many offspring programs that are either faster, more efficient, or more accurate than either of the two parents.

Logic and Fuzzy Logic

Regardless of the technique that is used to perform certain AI functions, most software is created using complex mathematical logic. A common symbolic logic system used in computer programming was developed in the mid-1800s by mathematician George Boole, and many search engines today use Boolean operators—AND, NOT, and OR—to logically locate appropriate information. Boolean logic is a way to describe sets of objects or information. For example, in Boolean logic:

Strawberries are red is true.

Strawberries are red AND oranges are blue is false.

Strawberries are red OR oranges are blue is true.

Strawberries are red AND oranges are NOT blue is true.

Boole's logic system fit well into computer science because all information could be reduced to either true or false and could be represented in the binary number system of 0s and 1s—with true being represented by a zero, and false by the number one, or vice versa.

Computers tend to view all information as black or white, true or false, on or off. But not everything in

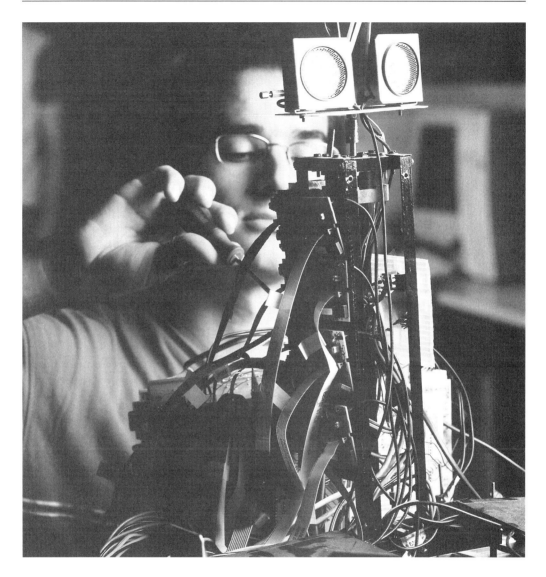

life follows the strict true-false, if-then logic. In the 1960s mathematician Dr. Lotfi Zadeh of the University of California at Berkeley developed the concept of fuzzy logic. Fuzzy logic systems work when hard and fast rules do not apply. They are a means of generalizing or softening any specific theory from a crisp and precise form to a continuous and fuzzy form.

Programs that forecast the weather, for example, deal in fuzzy logic. A fuzzy logic system understands

Computer scientist Alfonso Perez modifies Fuzzy Cat, a robot that uses fuzzy logic, a form of reasoning that works when hard and fast rules do not apply.

air temperature as being partly hot rather than being either hot or cold, and the temperature is expressed in the form of a percentage. Fuzzy logic programs are used to monitor the temperature of the water inside washing machines, to control car engines, elevators, and video cameras, and to recognize the subtle differences in written and spoken languages.

Alien Intelligence

Although traditional expectations of artificial intelligence are to duplicate human intelligence, author and computer specialist James Martin believes that that expectation is unrealistic. He believes that in the future AI should more properly be called alien intelligence, because the way computers "think" is vastly different from the way a human thinks.

AI is faster and has a larger capacity for storage and memory than any human. The largest nerves in the brain can transmit impulses at around 90 meters per second, whereas a fiber optics connection can transmit impulses at 300 million meters per second, more than 3 million times faster. A human neuron fires in one-thousandth of a second, but a computer transistor can fire in less than one-billionth of a second. The brain's memory capacity is some 30 billion neurons, while the data warehouse computer at Wal-Mart has more than 168 trillion bits of storage with the capacity to grow each year. Such a computer can process vast amounts of data that would bury a human processor and can quickly find patterns invisible to the human eye. The logical processes that some systems go through are so complex that even the best programmers cannot understand them. These computers, in a sense, speak a language that is understood only by another computer. Martin suggests that AI researchers of the past, who predicted a robot in every kitchen, promised more than could be delivered. But what they did create is much more than anyone could have dreamed possible.

Chapter 3

Everyday AI

The real success of AI is that most people are simply unaware of how significantly it affects and enables the routines of daily life. A man gets up in the morning to the smell of coffee already brewing. This is thanks to a microchip inside the coffee machine that allows him to program his coffeemaker to turn itself on while he is still sleeping. Another microchip keeps his toast from burning and remembers which setting from light to dark he likes best.

At one time these were all novel forms of AI. According to Douglas Hofstadter, a German researcher, "Once some mental function is programmed, people soon cease to consider it as an essential ingredient of 'real thinking.' AI is whatever hasn't been done yet."[8] Now that these features are commonplace, they are thought of as just another necessary product that makes life easier.

Already there are ovens on the market that keep food chilled until it starts to cook at a preset time. There are refrigerators with Web pads embedded in the doors to display recipes or to surf the Internet. The company iRobot now manufactures a robotic vacuum cleaner that buzzes around a room without a human operator.

But AI in the home today offers just a glimpse of what future household appliances will look like. "Most people don't realize fundamental changes in kitchen gear are coming. But in a decade or so, they won't know how they lived without their e-kitchens,"[9] says

The Roomba Intelligent Floorvac simplifies daily living by cleaning household floor surfaces at the touch of a button.

Bob Lamson, vice president of a company that makes high-tech gear. In the future, a cook may be able to place the ingredients on the kitchen counter and a built-in computer sensor will suggest recipes on the basis of those ingredients. Before leaving for work, a parent might place a frozen casserole in the oven and program it to defrost the casserole, then keep the dish chilled until it is time to start cooking. If traffic is tied up, the harried cook might simply be able to call the oven from the cell phone and reprogram the oven to delay dinner an hour. After dinner, family members might entertain themselves with one of the most sophisticated examples of AI in the home by playing a computer game.

Computer Games

Traditionally, AI computer programs have worked in the background, making sure that the digital environment of forests, smoking volcanoes, and rambling paths run smoothly. But AI is also used to make computer games more challenging for their human participants.

Most games are rule-based, which means that the computerized characters such as enemy guards, friendly wingmen, or monsters follow a basic set of rules according to what is happening around them. For example, if an enemy guard encounters a monster, it will attack the creature. If the creature flees, the enemy guard will chase after it, and if the enemy guard is fired on, it will dodge the bullet, spear, or laser ray. But these behaviors can become predictable for an experienced human player. By using AI, the computerized characters become less predictable and more difficult to overcome. Many designers incorporate fuzzy logic into the characters' decision-making programs so that the set of rules they operate under are less severe. All of the criteria do not have to be present for a character to act. There is flexibility in its behavior responses. Others use random weighting of certain attributes in order to create a more unanticipated chain of events.

More sophisticated games use AI software to analyze their human player's style of play. These programs actually learn to refine the game characters' social interactions so they can adapt to the human player's behavior. A game called Black and White God, designed by Richard Evans at Lionhead Studios, uses what he calls empathic learning to achieve this. In this game, if the human player throws fireballs at a tribal village, the computerized companion creature will learn that the player does not like the tribe. It will then act accordingly and spontaneously try to attack and stomp on that village's tribesmen.

Other games are goal based, which means that the computerized characters' behavior is determined by a larger preprogrammed goal. In Civilization III, by Firaxis Games, a player and various computer opponents fight military, economic, and cultural battles. The computerized opposition's goal is to stop the spread of the player's civilization by any means at their disposal. The characters' actions change depending on the obstacles put in their path.

Some of the most popular games are open-ended. Their characters do not have a finite path to follow or an ultimate goal. The top-selling game *The Sims* features a world of autonomous simulated people in an open-ended game where the human player oversees all the action. The characters, or Sims, interact based on a set of simple needs like food or entertainment. But the intelligence to interact with objects in the environment is not built into the Sims themselves. In a novel twist in programming, the objects in the environment advertise their ability to satisfy certain needs to any Sim character that is wandering by. The designer, Will Wright of Electronic Arts, calls this programming smart terrain. For example, when a Sim is looking around for fun, it may spot a beach ball. The Sim registers the beach ball's ability to satisfy its entertainment need. Wright explains, "All the instructions about how to bounce the ball are there as part of the ball's code."[10]

Rather than taking more control over a game's design, game designers are giving more control to the human player. Software called middleware can be downloaded and used to direct certain aspects of the game. A player can make the game harder or easier to play. For example, the precise noise level that would normally activate an enemy guard's attack pattern can be tuned up or down so that a softly creaking door would not alert the guard, but a weapon firing nearby would give the player away.

All of these unique AI programs, originally designed for mindless popular entertainment, are finding their

way into the hands of the military for use in training videos and simulated war games used to predict the outcome of battles. But they are also used in the movies. Paul Kruszewki, president of BioGraphic Technologies in Montreal, says, "The film people want intelligent extras."[11]

Software designer Will Wright created the popular computer game The Sims, *which features autonomous simulated people.*

A-Life in Hollywood

Some crowd scenes in animated movies are created with computers and made more realistic with AI. Called artificial life or A-life, the process involves using a computer to mimic groups of living things. The artificial life forms follow a set of rules that govern a group of living creatures. A simplistic example would look like a piece of graph paper or a chessboard. A few of the squares would each contain a creature called a cellular automaton, which is governed by a basic set of rules. One rule might be that a creature with fewer than two neighbors dies. Another might be that a group of three creatures produces one new creature. The program is set into motion with the rules in place and the colony of A-life creatures multiplies, dies, and changes from generation to generation. A new generation occurs each time the computer analyzes what has happened and calculates the automata's new positions.

More sophisticated A-life look like primitive creatures milling about on a computer screen, chasing each other, hunting for food, mating, or fighting. In the movies A-life characters may appear in the pastel colors of animated fairy-tale characters in a Disney crowd scene or with the gruesome heads and bodies of a Middle Earth Orc, a character in the *Lord of the Rings* trilogy.

A-Life Animation

A self-generating animation can be created by programming steering behaviors into each of the creatures in a group. This technique has been used to generate scenes of dancing villagers, stampeding herds, and schools of fish.

In a simple animation program of coordinated motion, each individual creature is programmed to:

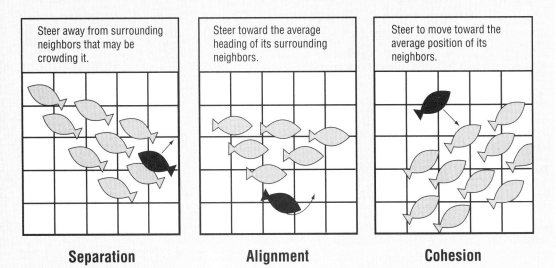

| Steer away from surrounding neighbors that may be crowding it. | Steer toward the average heading of its surrounding neighbors. | Steer to move toward the average position of its neighbors. |

Separation   **Alignment**   **Cohesion**

A-life programs allow the crowd of animated dancers in the final scene of *Shrek II* (2004) to move and twirl according to a set of guidelines that prevent them from bumping into each other. In early versions of the climax scene of the epic *Lord of the Rings* trilogy movie *Return of the King* (2003) the A-life forces of enemy Orcs kept running away. Each of the two hundred thousand computerized soldiers had been programmed to assess what was happening around them by drawing on their repertoire of military moves to fight the enemy. Unfortunately the A-life Orcs were smart enough to know they stood a better chance by dropping their weapons and fleeing. The A-life animators had to reprogram the Orcs specifically so they would stand and fight.

A-life technology is prominently featured throughout the computer-animated film Shrek II.

Driving AI

After seeing a movie, a family may hop into the car and again be confronted with more applications of AI at work. Electronic sensors throughout the car's engine monitor its efficiency. A neural network computer chip in newer models reduces the car's emissions and improves fuel efficiency by monitoring fuel combustion. Designed by the National Aeronautics and Space Administration's (NASA's) Jet Propulsion Laboratory, the chip can learn how to diagnose misfiring faster and alert the driver to engine problems.

In the 1990s, the U.S. Department of Transportation introduced the Intelligent Vehicle Initiative as part of the Transportation Efficiency Act for the 21st Century. Its mission is to look for ways to design cars and trucks that would prevent accidents and fatalities on the road. AI labs around the country are experimenting with all sorts of prototype AI systems, such as collision warning devices that use computerized voice, sound, or light to alert the driver to a possible crash and voice-activated controls so that the driver only has to push a single voice activation button on the steering wheel and command "Radio on" or "Temperature seventy degrees." Heat-detecting devices similar to the military's night vision systems would display infrared images on the windshield to warn drivers of an obstacle in their path. Sensors on the front of the car would allow the cruise control to maintain a safe speed and distance between vehicles by slowing or accelerating as needed.

"Smart cars" already give drivers the ability to navigate using the OnStar satellite system, which also automatically notifies emergency crews when an airbag has been deployed. The 2004 Toyota Prius even has sensors that can unlock the door when the driver's hands are full and help a driver safely back up into a parking space.

E-Commerce

Today a person does not have to get into a car to go shopping, thanks to sophisticated AI applications and the Internet. In 1995 almost no businesses conducted their affairs over the Internet. But by the year 2003 business-to-consumer sales on the Internet exceeded $100 billion and business-to-business sales more than $3 trillion.

As online purchasing booms, companies compete to find ways to maintain the growth of e-commerce and maximize their own market share and profits. One way is with an AI program called a collaborating filter. This software lets companies analyze their customers' buying patterns. The online bookstore Amazon.com, for example, uses collaborating filters to compare a person's buying patterns with those of other customers. Amazon then makes friendly recommendations of products tailored to a customer's peer preferences and profile. For example, someone who bought the latest Harry Potter novel may be offered a selection of books by the author Eoin Colfer, whose books are similar to J.K. Rowling's series. That suggestion is based on the knowledge that thousands of other people had previously purchased both. Even if a person does not buy online, the collaborative filtering engine keeps track of what products a person calls up on the viewing screen, so a buyer's potential purchases become part of the record.

Now when a person calls a company or logs on to a company's Web site, it is rare to actually contact a human being. Instead many businesses are relying on automated help desks that use an artificial intelligence system called case-based reasoning that works to match up the customer's problem to similar problems stored in its memory. It can then adapt a solution that worked in the past to the current problem.

But bypassing human-to-human interaction entirely has proven to have negative effects for businesses as well. Many people find computerized systems annoying and even alienating. A company called Extempo Systems in California seeks to alleviate this problem by offering so-called Expert Characters to guide a person through a Web site or a learning program. These

This female Chatterbot is designed to interact intelligently with people who visit her Web site.

Expert Characters, or Chatterbots, are digital characters who act like people and speak in a natural conversational style. They converse, listen, and interact, offering advice and guidance. Some Chatterbots will greet you when you visit a Web site and will even remember your product preferences from the last encounter.

AI in Business

AI is not just found in e-commerce. Expert systems help run most of the major businesses the world over. Wal-Mart harnesses an expert system enhanced with an ANN to sift through the data of all the sales at more than three thousand stores to find patterns and relationships between stores, products, and customers. It can find the pattern in what sells and what does not faster than hundreds of human analysts can. Expert systems even manage billions of dollars in the stock market.

The former editor of the *Wall Street Journal*, William Peter Hamilton, was a whiz at predicting movements in the stock market. His investment instincts beat the market by nearly 3 percentage points every year between 1930 and 1997. There was only one catch: Hamilton died in 1929! All of his amazing predictions were based on his knowledge but were produced by VirtualHamilton, another ANN expert system. A team of computer programmers mined Hamilton's writings to replicate his mindset. Then they fed the Virtual-

Hamilton seventy years of market data to see how it would perform. It was a hit. Now more than $250 billion is managed using AI stock market software.

Another stock market strategy involves sophisticated genetic algorithms. The program starts by generating millions of sets of rules for buying and selling stock. The ones that beat the market go on to multiply and mutate to become better, while those that cannot beat the market are killed off. This is done millions of times over until those that survive are the best methods of buying and selling stock.

ANN expert systems are used not only to make money but to save money. The artificial neural networks compare existing patterns to previous situations and eventually "learn" what works and what does not as the program digests more and more data. They also can seek out connections between data that a human programmer may not have thought of. For this reason they are most useful in detecting credit and insurance fraud. According to the magazine *Business Week*, these ANN expert systems have slashed the incidents of credit card fraud by 70 percent for major credit companies. A credit card applicant's buying habits, income, number of children, and residence are fed into the system. The system is also given a description of the type of customers who have committed credit card fraud. Over time, as patterns change, the ANN expert system adapts and follows the new patterns that emerge to highlight those customers who are a good credit risk and those who are not.

The Digital Doctor

Expert systems are also used in medicine to help doctors diagnose patients. In a 1997 study researchers concluded that medical students learn more than 47,000 facts and 29,000 concepts in just the first two years of medical school. Ideally all of that knowledge can be programmed into an expert system.

One diagnostic expert system, MYCIN, helps diagnose certain blood infections. MYCIN was tested for accuracy by comparing it with diagnoses of five prestigious staff members of the Stanford School of Medicine. The doctors were each given ten case histories and asked to diagnose the patients on paper and give their recommendations. Researchers found that the MYCIN expert system performed significantly better than the human panel!

Other types of artificial intelligence are being used in medical research. Special machines that have been dubbed robot scientists can formulate hypotheses, design experiments, and interpret the results as well as human scientists can. Packed with sophisticated robotics so that they can pick up and mix test tubes filled with liquids, these machines are networked to several computers programmed with advanced AI.

Another AI medical machine scans biopsy slides normally viewed under a microscope by a technician. The tissue samples are checked for the appearance of abnormal cells that may signal cancer. A trained human technician can look at hundreds of slides a day, but a trained machine is able to view thousands more, working nonstop all day and all night. It automatically stores images of the most suspicious cells for human technicians to review and double-check. X-rays are checked in the same way. Technicians that use AI software in X-ray scanners have improved their detection rates to 90 percent or better. Researchers working on the Human Genome Project also use AI software to tease out the millions of molecules of genetic code.

From performing the most sophisticated medical tests to making the simplest cup of coffee, AI is there. When coupled with robotics, AI is even more impressive. One life-saving surgical tool called the Pathfinder is a robotic arm that can be programmed to perform brain surgery. Its movements are so precise that even a surgeon with the steadiest hands cannot duplicate them.

This sleek and petite robotic arm is a distant cousin to the much larger hydraulic robotic arms that are used in automobile assembly plants. The sophisticated robotics technology that now makes a surgeon's job easier and more precise got its start welding car parts on the floor of a Detroit factory in the 1950s. From that humble beginning, the science and engineering of robotics have taken many shapes and been incorporated even more into people's lives.

A researcher working on the Human Genome Project loads data into a DNA sequencer that uses AI software.

Chapter 4

AI and Robotics

In 1958 Joseph Engelberger created the first robots—called Unimates—for factory work. They looked nothing like the fictional robots in movies or books; they looked more like giant flexing arms. The robots were hydraulically powered and programmed to move in a repeated pattern with exacting precision. Automobile manufacturers soon replaced assembly line workers with Unimates, which could perform the most exacting and physically demanding tasks.

A person who picks up a hammer and pounds in a nail does not think about the distance between his hand and the hammer or what force is needed. That mathematical and geometric calculation is immediate and unconscious. But that process must be hardwired into industrial robot computers so that mechanical movements are precise.

These giant arms are dangerous machines that swivel, swing, hammer, and weld with great force as partially assembled cars move past them. The welding arm must create strong, perfect seams to connect large metal panels on the assembly line. First it must analyze the alignment with its laser vision system. If it detects a misalignment, the robotic arm adjusts the pieces so that they line up correctly. Then it welds them to create the strongest bond possible. This kind of repetitive and precise work is perfectly suited for an

AI machine that does not cough, sneeze, blink, or get tired and make a mistake during welding.

Today robotic arms are used in almost every type of industry. They are especially useful in places where humans risk injury to themselves or their product. Smaller arms, for example, are used in the sterile environment of a silicon chip factory, where human workers wear special head-to-toe coveralls so that dandruff, flaking skin cells, and dirt do not contaminate the product. Industrial robotic arms work safely with toxic materials and perform their tasks in nuclear reactors and other dangerous places humans cannot go.

The Ford Motor Company invested nearly $700 million to equip its Flatrock, Michigan, plant with an assembly line of robotic arms.

But these AI arms are not versatile. Hand a robotic welding arm a screwdriver and it is useless. Unless reprogrammed, the industrial arm cannot adapt to another tool or task, but that versatility may come in the future. In the 1960s AI experts promised a robotic maid in every home. That has not happened, but AI experts are optimistic that it will. "A hundred years ago, we couldn't even fly, and now we have spacecraft exploring our solar system and beyond," says Tucker Balch, a computer scientist at Georgia Institute of Technology. "I think we're going to see just as radical a change in robots in the next century."[12] Already robotics and AI researchers are moving beyond the robotic arm to create intelligence in moving machines of all shapes and sizes. So far, some of the most successful and intriguing designs mimic nature.

Mechanical Animals on the Move

Using living creatures as inspiration for machines is called biomimicry. One of the leading scientists in the field is Robert J. Full of the University of California at Berkeley. He has never designed or built a robot, but he provides robot researchers with blueprints that come from the animal world. These blueprints may later be incorporated into various robot prototypes. Full gets his ideas from ghost crabs, ants, cockroaches, centipedes, and geckos.

As a biologist, Full studies the principles of animal locomotion. While cockroaches run on miniature treadmills, Full measures the electrical impulses in the insects' muscles with tiny electrodes and videotapes their movements with high-speed cameras. He details the locomotion movement by movement and documents the forces and dynamics involved. The information that he uncovers is then used to create some of the most mobile robots in the world that will be used for both civilian and military purposes. His work with the gecko, a sticky-toed lizard that can scurry up vertical surfaces, has led the company iRobot to create the Mecho-gecko, a small sensor-laden device that can cling to a wall and walk across the ceiling.

And for a robot, it seems that the more legs it has, the better. Full's analysis of cockroach movements has been used by researchers at Stanford University to build insectoid robots that scurry along the ground. Like the real insect, the insectoid robot moves along using two alternating sets of legs (two legs on one side; one leg on the other) as springs. And a crablike robot called Ariel wades sideways into the water and walks along the bottom of a pond.

In a giant tank of water at MIT, a robotic fish swims freely. Its creator believes it can be used to detect contamination in water reservoirs. If its sensors detect chemicals that should not be there, the robot can surface and transmit an alarm signal to the control center. Knowing that a fish with its slim muscles and small fins can accelerate at a rate of eight to twelve g's—as fast as a rocket—scientists hope to make better underwater propulsion systems too.

NASA is working on a robot shaped like a snake that will be able to slither into crevices, crawl into holes, and climb over the most rugged terrain without toppling like many wheeled vehicles. The snakebot, first developed by Mark Yim at Xerox Palo Alto Research Center, is made up of thirty hinged modules linked together in a chain. A central computer is located in the snakebot's head module, and smaller sensors and computers operate in each module throughout the body. The snakebot can sidewind, slither, and crawl like an inchworm. It can also coil up to grasp a tool or flip over obstacles. NASA hopes this style of robot will help on future missions to Mars. Added sensors and adaptive learning software will make it one of the more self-sufficient robots to go into space.

In Japan, scientists at Nagoya University have moved robots up the evolutionary ladder to create a monkeylike robot. Shaped like a gangly gibbon, this robot can hang and swing from bars suspended from

Left: *Using bio-mimicry, engineers created this spiderbot capable of negotiating difficult terrain.*

Right: *NASA hopes to use this hopping frogbot to explore distant planets, comets, and asteroids.*

the ceiling. Video cameras track its movement, and every time it makes a mistake, it has to learn how to correct it and try again. Called Brachiator III (*brachiate* means "to swing"), it is almost as agile and quick as a real monkey.

Motor Intelligence

Each complex movement that a robot makes to mimic the swish of a fin, the swing of an arm, or a slither of a snake involves some form of AI. These movements can be made only with the right kind of programming. Joseph Ayers of Northeastern University says, "The same basic organizational units of the nervous system are involved in the motor systems of all animals. If you know how to use that architecture, you should be able to build a robot to operate in any environment on the planet."[13] Understanding the motor intelligence of animals helps researchers build more sophisticated robots.

Many robotic animals operate with low-level behaviors. When such a robot perceives a situation through its sensors, it responds with a fixed set of behaviors. For example, when a robot encounters a rock, it is programmed to crawl over it. If the rock is large

On future expeditions to Mars, NASA hopes to send snakebots like this one that are capable of slithering into crevices and crawling into holes.

and the robot tries to crawl over it as usual, the robot might topple over instead. With the help of motor intelligence, AI robotic experts are layering on adaptive learning behaviors so that the responses are no longer fixed. With higher level behaviors, a robot would sense the large rock and respond based on a repertoire in its memory. If it attempted to crawl around the rock and was successful, that connection between the sensors and the response would be strengthened. The next time the robot encountered a similar-sized object, it would know to crawl around it. AI software is the connection between what is perceived by the robot and the robot's response.

Robot Explorers

Why mimic nature? Researchers hope these designs will be able to go where humans cannot go and do what humans cannot do. Robots do not need oxygen to breathe; they do not get claustrophobic or feel pain. Crab robots can blend into the seabed and patrol underwater for hours. The military hopes they can be used for detecting underwater mines. Insectoid robots can crawl into the tiniest spaces, like into small pipes or inside a wall, and snakebots can slither into cracks and crevices. But not all robotic explorers look like animals. Some resemble tiny tanks or golf carts.

In 1994 an eight-legged robot was sent clambering into the steaming caldera of Mount Spurr in Alaska. Called Dante II, the robot explorer took air samples and allowed scientists to view, for the first time, the active volcano via a remote-controlled video camera. A similar Dante robot made by Red Whittaker at Carnegie Mellon Institute also hunted for meteorites in frigid Antarctica.

These machines also protect human workers from toxic levels of radiation. When the Chernobyl nuclear power plant blew up in April 1986, it released four hundred times more radioactive waste than the U.S. bombing of Hiroshima. The radioactive building and all of its contents has been sealed off in a cement sarcophagus ever since. In 1996 a robot named Pioneer was sent in to map the interior, collect samples, and inspect for leaks. Less than four feet tall, Pioneer was narrow enough to fit through doorways, strong enough to bulldoze through piles of debris, yet agile enough to pick up samples of radioactive waste and water.

A shoebox-sized robot with tanklike treads helped archaeologists explore previously unknown parts of the Great Pyramid at Giza in Egypt. It climbed a tiny airshaft of the forty-five-hundred-year-old pyramid and inched along more than two hundred feet before coming to a door made of plaster. When the robot poked its camera though the plaster, it discovered . . . another door!

Into tiny airshafts, hot lava, or freezing ice, robots are capable of going anywhere, even into outer space. On January 3, 2004, the first of two NASA rovers landed safely on Mars and began to explore the surface of the Red Planet. These two rovers, Spirit and Opportunity, are identical robotic vehicles about the size of golf carts. Riding on six wheels, the rovers' sturdy bodies contain all they need to survive for three months. Their computer systems monitor their health to make sure the insides do not get overheated during the hot Mars day and do not freeze during the cold nights. Each is equipped with X-ray, infrared spectrometry, microscopes, and other geological instruments to collect soil and rock samples and test for evidence of water. Spirit and Opportunity are not the first robots on Mars. The smaller Sojourner explored Mars in 1997. It was the first time an intelligent robot was able to react to unplanned events on the surface of another planet. Sojourner had been on the planet only a few days when its hazard avoidance system switched on and it had to make its own decisions about where to go without any internal mapping information.

Researchers test the Pyramid Rover, which they designed to explore previously unknown parts of Egypt's Great Pyramid of Giza.

Search-and-Rescue Robots

When the twin towers of the World Trade Center were destroyed on September 11, 2001, robotics expert Robin Murphy and three colleagues from the University of South Florida drove eighteen hours to New York City to help search through the rubble for survivors. They brought eight different search-and-rescue

This search-and-rescue robot is used for transporting hoses to fire fighters and locating people in need of rescue from burning buildings.

robots with them. The most successful was a miniature tank with treads that crawled into voids thirty
feet deep. Although the robots did not discover any
survivors, they did prove their usefulness. They could
get into spaces that men and rescue dogs could not,
and the thick dust in the air did not hamper their ol-
factory sensors, as it did some of the rescue dogs.

Since the terrorist attack, robotics experts and rescue workers from the Federal Emergency Management
Agency (FEMA) have collaborated on designing better search-and-rescue robots. Recently FEMA crews
blew up an empty building in order to test different
models of robots and learn what works and what does
not. Even small adjustments, like making the joystick
controls large enough to manipulate with gloved
hands, made a difference in the robot's effectiveness.
"Until you experience a rescue operation, it's hard to
understand the real rescue questions that must be addressed for this technology to be transferred to search-
and-rescue users,"[14] says Robin Murphy, the director
of the Center for Robot-Assisted Search and Rescue at
the University of South Florida. These robots are
equipped with infrared sensors that detect body heat,
night vision, and cameras that search for colors dis-
tinctive from the gray dust that blankets a site. Any
speck of color, such as that of blood or fabric, is easily identified.

Another important part of rescue missions and
worker safety is knowing secure routes to take. In 2002
nine miners became stranded in a flooded mine in
Somerset, Pennsylvania, by following a flawed map
that did not show how dangerously close they were
to a flooded mine shaft. In response to this crisis a new
kind of robot was created to assist miners in mapping
out safe routes in real time. The mapmaker is a small
robot called Groundhog. Scientists at Carnegie Mellon
equipped Groundhog with cameras; gas, tilt, and sink-
age sensors; laser scanners; and a gyroscope. The robot can map out mine shafts as it moves through them

using sensor data processed through AI software called Simultaneous Localization and Mapping, or SLAM. Groundhog successfully mapped a thirty-five-hundred-foot Pennsylvania mine shaft in May 2003.

Warbots

Many search-and-rescue robots and animal robots are products of research and development programs sponsored in part by the U.S. military. The Defense Advanced Research Projects Agency (DARPA) hopes that in the future whole schools of robotic fish will patrol shipping channels looking for sunken mines, and a patrol of Mecho-geckos equipped with cameras and audio equipment can be sent up the side of a sky-scraper to peek into windows and assess the situation inside. According to military robotics pioneer Scott D. Myers, "Military robots are being developed and fielded to do three things: perform the dull, the dirty and the dangerous."[15]

With an increased focus on counteracting terrorist attacks, the Pentagon is paying closer attention to machines that perform dangerous missions and keep people out of harm's way. In 2002 U.S. soldiers in Afghanistan used robots to explore caves before the troops were sent in. The Packbot, which looks like a miniature flattened tank, runs on treads and has flipperlike arms that allow it to crawl over anything. It is sturdy enough to be thrown through a window, climb up stairs, and fall from the balcony and still be fully operational. During Operation Iraqi Freedom in 2003, a squad of Packbots searched tunnels under the Baghdad airport to look for enemy soldiers thought to be hiding out and examined equipment left on an airfield that was believed to be booby-trapped.

A state-of-the-art unmanned reconnaissance airplane called Predator can cruise at twenty-five thousand feet for more than five hundred miles and can stay aloft for up to twenty minutes. Controlled by a pilot on the ground using a joystick, the small Predator can relay back information about the location of enemy troops and weather conditions, leaving troops safe on the ground.

According to Colonel Tommy Dillard, Airforce Battlelab commander, "One of the things we have asked [the robotics] industry to do is to be able not only to detect [intruders] with robots, but to start a neutralization phase before we get response forces out there."[16] Robotics experts have created robots that can detonate suspect packages in an airport or on a crowded street in Baghdad. Small robotic guard units equipped with a range finder, motion detectors, a communication system, and weapon can locate and track an intruder, call for backup, and even fire a gun.

The Race for Unmanned Vehicles

In 2001 the U.S. Congress mandated that one-third of military ground vehicles be unmanned by the year 2015. That means they should be able to navigate, steer, and respond to various situations without the help of a driver. The parts needed for such a vehicle are advanced laser, radar, and sonar sensor systems to help the vehicle navigate, and Global Positioning System (GPS) to plot its location. So far all the components have not been assembled to create a workable machine that can maneuver across rocky terrain on its own. One prototype, called Navlab II, is a U.S. Army truck driven by a computer called ALVINN (Autonomous Land Vehicle in a Neural Network). Its computer steering algorithms allow it to drive without a driver, and basic pattern recognition systems allow the vehicle to recognize and follow the lines of a road. But an off-road situation is completely different. Dodging a boulder in the path would be fairly easy for Navlab II, but having the vehicle determine whether the obstacle was a boulder or a tumbleweed is more difficult.

To help the military achieve a truly autonomous vehicle, DARPA organized a contest to build the world's first truly autonomous robotic land vehicle. Teams of professional robotics engineers, individual garage

In 2001 robotic engineers designed autonomous robotic vehicles like this one to compete in the DARPA Grand Challenge race in California.

tinkerers, and one high school science club vied for the $1 million prize. The crew from Palos Verdes High School called themselves the Road Warriors, and they reconfigured a sports utility vehicle donated by Honda. One lone graduate student tried to make a motorcycle that could get around roadblocks, zip down tight alleyways, and be parachuted into a city. A team of college graduate students worked on a giant Humvee. To win the million-dollar prize, the vehicle had to be able to cross a specific 210-mile course through the desert from Los Angeles to Las Vegas within ten hours. The army's Future Combat Systems program was hoping that the robotics contest would produce a winner, but so far no vehicle has finished the course. The contest will be held again in 2005.

However, large corporations like Lockheed and United Defense Industries may cross the finish line first. United Defense Industries is working on an armed robotic vehicle with missiles and gun turrets to provide targeting information for other weapons and to drop miniature sensors onto the battlefield. Another vehicle still in the research stage is called the Soldier Unmanned Ground Vehicle (SUGV). Operated by remote control, it will be small enough to climb stairs and use its sensor devices to see around corners during urban combat. The SUGV is also being fitted with a grenade launcher, directional microphones, and motion detectors, which would allow it to stand sentry while soldiers sleep.

All of this AI robotic technology is meant to keep soldiers out of harm's way. Many people suspect that the idea of a platoon of robotic soldiers, reminiscent of a *Star Wars* movie, is the inevitable next step.

Chapter 5

In Pursuit of
the Mechanical
Man

Robot soldiers in any form may be decades away, but that task is simple compared with the skills and efforts needed to produce a robot that could be mistaken for a real human. Creating a humanoid robot is the ultimate goal for many AI researchers, and the most daunting. A convincing humanoid robot would have to walk, gesture, and maneuver as easily as a human, understand the spoken language, be able to communicate, and perhaps even be able to feel emotions and respond to feelings. These are just some of the challenges that AI researchers in labs all over the world must consider.

The scientific research in pursuit of the mechanical man is scattered. Researchers tend to specialize in only one small area of humanoid robotic operation such as speech recognition, visual perception, or mobility, each of which is a highly technical, complex discipline in itself. This is an enormously costly endeavor with an uncertain timeline. For many years, Japan has led the research in humanoid robotics because, as Hirohisa Hirukawa of Japan's National Institute of Advanced Industrial Science and Technology says, "We are confident that the long-term future of humanoid robots is bright."[17]

Why Make It Look Human?

Researchers already know how to make machines that are sturdy enough to be dropped onto another planet, smart enough to run businesses, and precise enough to perform surgery. So why would scientists go to all the trouble of making a robot look like a person? This question is hotly debated. Some scientists believe there is no reason. So far, nonhumanoid robots perform better than those with humanoid designs, and it is less expensive to create machines that maneuver on several legs or on wheels or treads. Some researchers raise ethical concerns that if robots look too human there may be the potential for abuse. "Robots need to be designed so that they will be regarded as appliances rather than as people,"[18] says John McCarthy of Stanford University. People may treat humanoid robots as slaves,

David Hanson sculpted humanlike features for his robotic head, Hertz, and programmed it to exhibit realistic facial expressions.

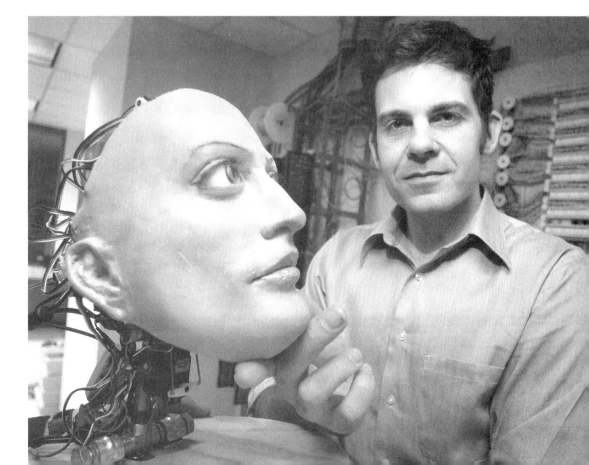

The Creep Factor

Kismet's face hardly resembles a human's, but it is cute and it does attract an observer's attention because of its lifelike expressions. David Hanson, who worked for Walt Disney Imaging as a sculptor-roboticist, is one researcher who is working on putting a more realistic face on future robots. He created a high-tech polymer plastic that resembles human skin, which he calls f'rubber. With it he created a very human-like face over a robotic head. So far powered only by a laptop computer, the head, called Hertz, can bat its eyes and ask questions. Hertz has twenty-eight very realistic-looking facial movements, including smiling, sneering, and furrowing its brow. But a robot who looks too real can cause problems. Tests showed that a robot with a face that was too realistic gave people the creeps and actually decreased the robot's effectiveness.

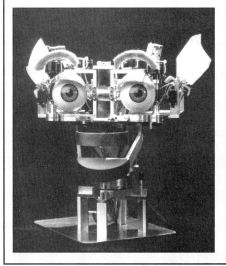

People find the robot Kismet's lifelike expressions cute, and not creepy at all, perhaps because Kismet does not resemble a human.

and that is one relationship that ethicists fear could carry over to interpersonal relationships.

The other side in this debate is strongly in favor of a robot that looks like a person, especially if it were to work with people in a home or work environment. "If you build a robot that people have a short-term interaction with, you'd better make it connect with things people are familiar with,"[19] says Stanford University professor Sebastian Thrun. People are more likely to interact with a robot that is designed like themselves than a robot with an alien shape and design. There is also the belief that the essence of intelligence is a combination of mind and body. Japanese robotics expert Fumio

Hara believes that a robot would not be completely effective without the embodiment of a humanlike presence. So what elements are essential in order to make a robot humanlike? It needs to have a familiar face, identifiably humanlike behaviors, appropriate social interactions, and of course a physical form that stands upright and is capable of walking on two legs.

Walk This Way

Almost all children are toddling around on two legs by the age of two. This physical attribute took millions of years to evolve in primates. Honda, one of the largest industrial companies in the world, spent millions of dollars but only ten years of top-secret research to effectively duplicate this movement in a machine.

Walking upright is extremely difficult to duplicate and requires a lot of AI computing power. It requires balance, coordination, muscle power, and flexibility just to take three steps across a smooth tile floor in a straight line. But stepping out into an unfamiliar rocky terrain with many obstacles in a robot's path requires even more AI power to adjust a step, alter foot placement, and register ground resistance—things people do without conscious thought.

Honda's robot, ASIMO (Advanced Step in Innovative Mobility), is able to walk backward and sideways, go up and down stairs, and even play soccer. ASIMO looks like a small child traipsing around in a white plastic space suit. ASIMO is only four feet tall, but it can simulate human locomotion and use its arms in a realistic fashion. Its designers made special efforts to make it cute so that it was not perceived as threatening and would be more easily accepted. In 2003 ASIMO marched into a state dinner attended by the prime ministers of Japan and the Czech Republic. ASIMO shook hands with Prime Minister Vladimir Spidla and placed a bouquet of flowers at the base of a statue honoring science fiction author Karel Capek, who coined the term *robot* in 1920.

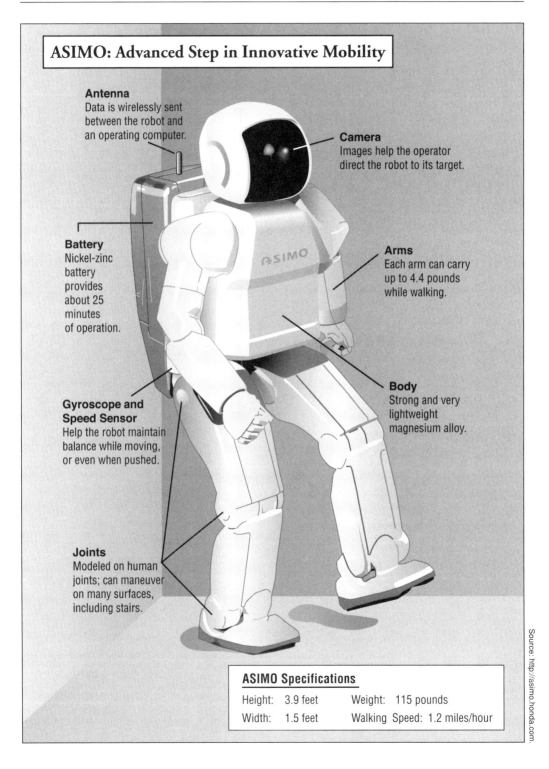

ASIMO: Advanced Step in Innovative Mobility

Antenna
Data is wirelessly sent between the robot and an operating computer.

Camera
Images help the operator direct the robot to its target.

Battery
Nickel-zinc battery provides about 25 minutes of operation.

Arms
Each arm can carry up to 4.4 pounds while walking.

Gyroscope and Speed Sensor
Help the robot maintain balance while moving, or even when pushed.

Body
Strong and very lightweight magnesium alloy.

Joints
Modeled on human joints; can maneuver on many surfaces, including stairs.

ASIMO Specifications

Height:	3.9 feet	Weight:	115 pounds
Width:	1.5 feet	Walking Speed:	1.2 miles/hour

Source: http://asimo.honda.com.

ASIMO is a tiny humanoid robot that can simulate human locomotion and can even play soccer.

Other humanoid robots have demonstrated their prowess at martial arts, soccer, dancing, and even conducting an orchestra. The key to making a robot athletic is simulating the muscle, bone, and nerves in machinery. All robots make use of many of the same components: a jointed metal or plastic skeletal frame and motors, pulleys, gears, and hydraulics to provide the muscle power. But advances in polymer chemistry are changing that. Researchers are experimenting with new materials such as EAP, or electroactive polymer, to produce more realistic muscle power. EAP is a rubbery plastic substance that works by changing shape when electricity is applied to it. It can be made into bundles of fibers that are able to shorten or lengthen, just like real muscles, when the fibers are attached to a motor. The material also weighs less and is less likely to break down than metal. But the most important element is the brainpower needed to coordinate it all.

ASIMO carries its computer brain in a pack on its back. It has three cameras (two on its head and one at its waist) that allow it to see and chase a soccer ball. It also has sensors in each ankle to predict its next step. Gravity sensors keep track of the force of each movement, and solid-state gyroscopes monitor its body position and keep it upright. But what keeps this petite robot upright and balanced while carrying out complex movements are impressive AI algorithms programmed into its circuitry. If ASIMO stands on one leg and swings its arm out to the side, the program automatically adjusts and the robot moves its torso to keep its balance.

Getting Around

Being able to move and walk on two legs is one accomplishment, but knowing how to navigate is another. Using preprogrammed maps like Shakey the robot used fifty years ago is no longer the way robots get around. Today genetic algorithms direct robotic navigation and control systems so that a robot can learn and adapt to any new environment. There are many navigation programs under experimentation, but the most unusual uses pain as a navigational tool.

Robots in this experiment were trained to seek out specific objects, grab them, and transport them to a specific drop-off point. The experiment's designer, Matthew Hage of the Lawrence Livermore National Laboratory, influenced the robot's choice of route by programming it to "feel" pain. When the robot bumped into a physical object, it "hurt" from the damage it suffered. If it came close to a hot spot, a place where radiation emanated, the robot also associated it with pain and kept its distance. The robot's task, then, was to follow the least painful path.

Sensory Perception

Few robots are equipped to perceive stimuli as pain, but sensory perception is key to making an effective humanoid robot or any other artificial intelligence. Humans experience the world through five senses. In order for a robot to interact with humans effectively, it has to be able to experience what humans experience. Without the senses of hearing, touch, sight, taste, and smell, people would not be able to act fully within their environment. Even Alan Turing felt that perception was important in his early theoretical design. In his paper "Computing Machinery and Intelligence" he suggested, "It is best to provide the machine with the best sense organs that money can buy and then teach it to understand and speak English. This process could follow the normal teaching of a child."[20]

Perception and thinking are the respective functional correlates of the sensory organs and the brain. In order to learn the most from its environment, the human brain fine-tunes how and what a person senses. Giving machines the chance to perceive the world through similar, if not better, sensory organs allows them a chance to understand the world as humans do. Otherwise they would simply be programmed machines incapable of learning.

Some of the earliest perception systems were designed to recognize language, that is, identify characters and words that make up text. Once the language was perceived, the machine would convert it into a coded form. For example, most search engines today operate using Optical Character Recognition Systems to read typed-in information. Understanding what that information meant, however, was limited to the context of the word or symbol. What at first looked like a simple exercise to create a machine that could see and recognize symbols became an exploration into how humans perceive and understand the world.

Artificial Vision

Many aspects of human sensory perception are difficult if not impossible to duplicate. The human eye, for example, is an incredibly complex structure that

With its four camera "eyes," Cog, an android developed at MIT, sees an object from four distinct perspectives.

provides frontal and peripheral vision; a pair of eyes also provides depth perception and better form recognition. The eyes can lock on to a moving object and follow it in one smooth motion or move in a stop and start motion from object to object so that vision is not blurry as a person's eyes move around. The eyes register the level of light and measure depth and distances of objects. The eyes sift through a lot of information before any encoded messages are sent to the brain, where 60 percent of the cerebral cortex is devoted to processing visual information. Scientists know how the eye operates—the mechanics of the eye and its movements can be duplicated—but scientists know much less about how eye-brain perception works. Duplicating that connection is more difficult.

To simulate eye-brain perception, a robot needs several cameras operating at the same time. The cameras must be connected to a neural network that can sift through data to pass on the pertinent information to higher levels of network. Mathematical algorithms convert patterns of color intensities and turn them into descriptions of what appears before the cameras. Computer vision is capable of detecting human faces, locating eyes in a face, tracking movement, and registering various shapes and colors. But it is not as good at recognizing whether a face is male or female, determining the direction of a person's gaze, or recognizing the same person who appears later with a hat or beard, or recognizing the difference between a cup and a comb. Those distinctions come from a higher level of perception that is still being explored. A robot's view of the world is best described by Rodney Brooks in his book *Flesh and Machines* as "a strange, disembodied, hallucinatory experience."[21]

Artificial Ears

Like eyes, ears are complex organs. The human ear is capable of registering and identifying thousands of different sounds. A person can determine what made the sound and how far away the source of the sound may have been. Microphones that operate as a robot's ears only receive the sound. The perception comes in the form of complex AI programs that register sound and match it to a stored catalog of recognizable noises.

Human ears receive sound in waves, which are converted into electrical impulses that are sent to the brain. This conversion is done in the cochlea of the ear, where the sound waves resonate and trigger the movement of tiny hairs called cilia, which fire the attached neural cells. An artificial ear operates in much the same way. Locating the origin of a sound is done through measuring the infinitesimal differences in time between the waves reaching two different microphones. Speech recognition is achieved through the use of sophisticated pattern recognition software.

Touch

The sense of touch is also very complicated. Large industrial robotic arms are dangerous when they maneuver with great force; a humanoid robot would need to have a delicate sense of touch so that if it bumped into a person, the robotic arm would recoil automatically without harming the human.

A humanoid robot would also have to be able to use human tools and grasp and hold objects. Robotic hands are designed with special strain gauges that measure the amount of pressure needed to pick up an object and contact switches that simulate touch and grasping motions. When a switch comes in contact with something, it closes and sends a signal to the computer brain. The strain gauges record the appropriate amount of pressure needed to pick up the object, making it possible for the same robotic hand to pick up a hammer one minute and a fragile egg the next.

NASA has engineered one of the more dexterous robots, called Robonaut, to perform dangerous construction work on the space station. The prototype had to be designed to use finer motor skills than a space-suited astronaut would have. Each arm attached to Robonaut's Kevlar body contains more than 150 sensors that are connected to an artificial spinal cord

Extrasensory Perception

The advantage of an artificial system is that it can be enhanced with extrasensory perception. For example, an artificial nose can be enhanced to far exceed the sensitivity of a flesh-and-blood nose. Called neural noses, these microchips are so sensitive that they can detect smells that humans are not even aware of. Artificial noses are used in airports to detect explosive materials and narcotics and may be used in diagnosing cancer by smelling precancerous tissues. Incorporating this type of extrasensory perception into a humanoid robot would give it an advantage over its human counterpart. Military robots, for example, might be fitted with chemical noses or infrared night vision that would tell them when a living being was nearby.

through which sensory signals flow quickly back and forth to the computer brain. Its hands are capable of opening a can of soda, cutting with scissors, and handling tools commonly used on the space station.

Researchers in Japan are also working on a way to make robot hands as sensitive as a human hand. A rubbery pressure-sensing membrane laminated onto a flexible layer of plastic transistors creates a primitive artificial skin. When the fake skin is touched with the metal tip of a rod, it generates a weak electrical signal, which is then sent to receivers in the computer brain and registers as a touch.

Educating Cog

A robot that can touch, see, and hear is ready to experience the world as a human does. One robot that embodies Alan Turing's idea of allowing a robot to learn like a child through sensory perception is Cog (from the Latin word *cogitare*, "to think"). A human infant learns through trial and error as it encounters each new aspect of its environment. Each new piece of information it learns is filed away and used as a basis for more experiences and learning opportunities. Cog, created at MIT more than ten years ago, learns the same way but is still no more knowledgeable than a six-month-old baby.

Unlike Deep Blue and other expert systems, Cog was not programmed to do much of anything. It must learn all the necessary data it needs by experiencing the world around it. It learns to move and react by watching its trainer's movements and reactions. Cog's bulky metal frame and face hide the fact that it is just a baby. Like an infant, it can track movement with its camera eyes and move its head to keep an object in view. It can recognize some faces, detect eye contact, and react to sounds.

This imitative learning takes time, but it is approaching self-directed learning because it allows interaction between human and robot. Cog can ask

Cog creator Rodney Brooks hopes that his android will teach researchers more about the way people learn by interacting with others.

questions or request that a movement be repeated over and over. Some robots have even shown frustration and boredom when the learning process gets difficult.

Emotions

Down the hall from Cog is its cousin, Kismet. Inspired by Cog's infantile behavior, researcher Cynthia Breazeal created Kismet, one of the most sociable robots. Whereas no one treats the hulkish Cog like a baby, people frequently use baby talk with Kismet. A cartoonish head bolted to a table, Kismet will respond to a person's approach, waggle its fuzzy, caterpillar-like eyebrows, and turn up its red licorice-whip lips in a grin. The underlying premise of Kismet is that emotions are necessary to guide learning and communication.

Because most information exchanged between humans is done through facial expressions, it is important to give a robot facial expressions to make robot-human interactions as informative as possible. A human infant will smile and try to attract the attention of its mother. When that is achieved, it will follow the mother's

Cynthia Breazeal programmed Kismet to communicate its moods through complex facial expressions.

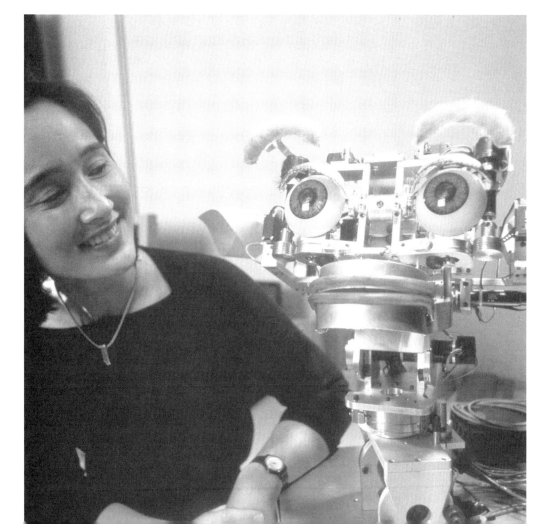

movements and try to engage in play. Kismet can do the same. As a baby is motivated by hunger or thirst, Kismet is motivated by stimulation. It is programmed with a social, or stimulation, drive, which means it seeks out experiences that will stimulate it. But it also has a fatigue syndrome, which means it gets tired over time. The goal is for Kismet to keep these two drives in balance and learn what works and what does not in social situations. "The robot is trying to get you to interact with it in ways that can benefit its ability to learn,"[22] says Breazeal.

For example, Kismet is programmed to seek out social stimulation. Its bright blue eyes are always looking around for movement, bright colors, skin tones, and face shapes. The images it takes in are processed through a neural network that recognizes faces and their expressions. Its large pink ears listen for voices. When it senses a person is near, it will try to attract the person with facial expressions and baby talk. If an expression works and a person passing by stops to talk, Kismet's internal social drive program is satisfied. If the expression does not work, the internal social drive level sinks and prompts Kismet to try something different. Kismet also knows how to react to stimulation it perceives negatively. If a person gets too close to its face, Kismet will sense an invasion of space and either mimic an expression of annoyance or turn away.

Breazeal programmed Kismet with a repertoire of seven basic facial movements, but she theorizes that the more Kismet interacts with humans, the more it will learn and refine those expressions and add to them. Its impressive array of facial expressions is controlled by fifteen external computers along one wall, with no one computer in control.

Putting All the Pieces Together

All of these components—bipedalism, sensory perception, and facial expressions—have yet to be put together into an effective and convincing mechanical

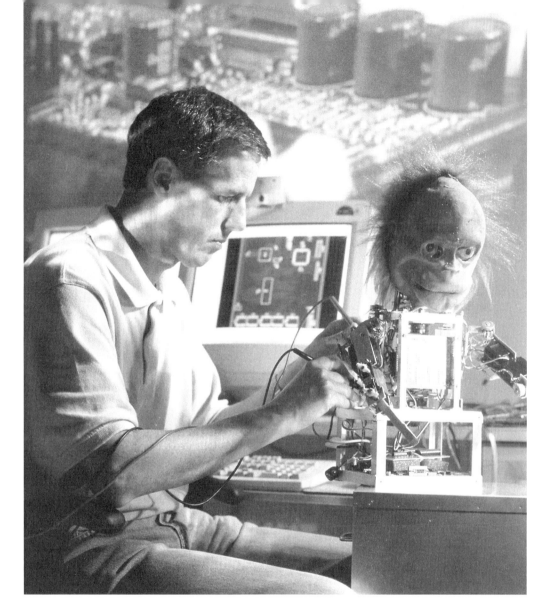

man. There are no robots that combine the mobility of ASIMO, the sociability of Kismet, and the chess-playing ability of Deep Blue. Many of the skills that humans take for granted like running, enjoying music, or recognizing objects are still beyond the abilities of even the most advanced robots, but AI researchers are working on them piece by piece. The potential is there. No one can determine a date in the future when humanoid robots will babysit children or assist the elderly, but hope is high and the technology is progressing.

British researcher Steve Grand built Lucy to test his theories about sensory perception and artificial intelligence.

Chapter 6

The Future of AI

A I of the future may not look like Cog or have the moves of ASIMO, but it will probably exhibit many of the same attributes that are being perfected in these humanoid robots. The science of artificial intelligence is less than sixty years old, which is young for a branch of science, yet AI has advanced phenomenally since the early days of moth-ridden vacuum tubes. The future of AI is hard to predict, but no one questions that it will be more available and more abundant and present in people's lives. Some experts anticipate that in the future AI hardware will become smaller, AI will become an essential element of caring for the elderly, and it will include a blending of the best of both human and mechanical intelligences.

Mini AI

The direction of all electronics and technology continues to be toward ever smaller and more portable products. The first generation of computers, giants that filled entire rooms with whirring gears and fans, gave way to desktop versions run by transistors. The technology shrank dramatically with the invention of silicon chips. Laptops have been miniaturized to handheld computers, and cell phones are half the size they were just five years ago. That trend is reflected in AI also.

A cutting-edge artificial intelligence technology being perfected at the University of California at Berkeley
works on an incredibly small scale. "Smart dust" is a
network of wireless micro-electromechanical sensors
the size of dust particles—imagine grains of sand with
a brain—that could monitor everything from temperature, light, vibration, and movement to radiation
and toxic chemicals. The particles of smart dust, called
motes, could be as small as one cubic millimeter,
which would fit on the tip of a ballpoint pen. At present, prototype smart dust motes are about the size of
a pager and run on AA batteries. But these sensors have

*A professor at
the University of
California at Berkeley
displays two energy-
conserving "smart
dust" sensors he
invented.*

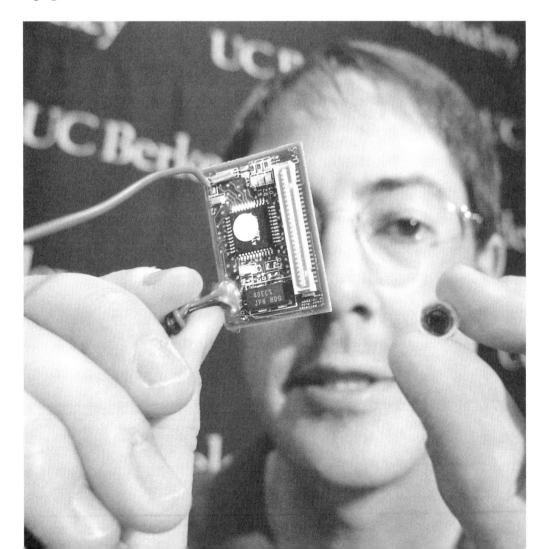

infinite possibilities. Scientists hope that these mini-sensors can be sprinkled throughout a large area like tiny dust motes floating in the air.

Networked by the hundreds, smart dust motes can pass information from one to the other almost instantaneously. They survey the world around them and "chat" wirelessly through the system until the information reaches a central computer. Smart dust is being marketed for use in factories, homes, and public places and for commercial, military, medical, security, and ecological applications. For example, sensors dispersed in an art gallery could sense movement when the gallery was closed. They could be placed anywhere inside or outside an active airport to detect chemical weapons or plastic explosives. Sensors dropped from an airplane could help predict the path of a forest fire,

Scientists envision medical nanorobots capable of traveling through the human bloodstream to target disease-causing agents.

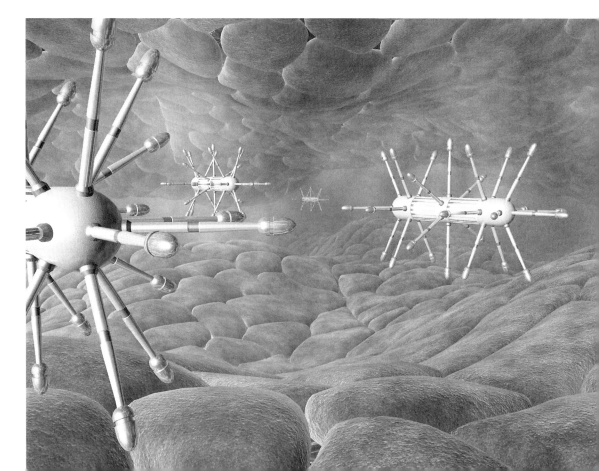

and those positioned around a house could monitor the vital signs of the people living inside.

Not quite as small as the proposed smart dust, but more mobile, is the microfly, a robot project funded by the Department of Defense. The microfly will weigh less than a paper clip and zip about on wings that are only one-twentieth the thickness of a sheet of paper. Its artificial intelligence sensors will allow it to run reconnaissance missions for the military and scout out enemy troops without being detected. According to Promode Bandyopadhyay, head of robotics at the federal Office of Naval Research, "You could have a swarm of them in a battlefield. Eventually, they can work as a group and detect the presence of hostile forces and materials."[23]

Writer and researcher Ray Kurzweil has predicted even smaller robotic AI systems using nanotechnology, which is the engineering of devices on a microscopic scale. He suggests that nanobots could be injected into the human body and travel through a person's system to detect disease. There already is such a device, developed in France, that is small enough to be swallowed. It moves along the patient's digestive tract and with a tiny wheel measures the intestines and takes samples. It can also be programmed to stop at a certain spot to release a dose of medicine or perform a simple surgical procedure. German researchers have devised an even smaller robotic unit that can travel inside a blood vessel. As thin as a matchstick, it has three moving sections that push and pull it along like an inchworm. An even smaller robotic arm has been created that is no bigger than a hyphen. Its tiny silicon frame can bend and grab glass beads only a fraction of an inch long.

Advances in powering such tiny AI robots have made surprising leaps in recent years. Some researchers are even using parts of bacteria to create tiny rotors similar to those of a helicopter or a propeller on a boat to move these micromachines along. So far these machines are not equipped with intelligence systems, but researchers believe that in the future they will be used to locate and destroy cancer cells and monitor human health.

Seniorbots

Monitoring health is an increasing concern in the U.S. medical community. Within fifty years, more than 30 percent of the population will be over the age of sixty-five, and the National Institute on Aging predicts that more than 14 million Americans will be diagnosed with Alzheimer's disease. With fewer caregivers and a growing population of potential patients, people will need other kinds of assistance to live happier, safer, and more independent lives. Companies that specialize in AI are scrambling to find ways to help. "Assisted cognition systems will enable aging adults to stay at home longer and to take care of themselves,"[24] says Eric Dishman from Intel Labs. Dr. Zeungnam Bien, director of the Robot Welfare Research Center, agrees: "Various forms of welfare robotic systems will be the means of sustaining society."[25]

In the home robotic aides will be able to open the refrigerator, retrieve a jar, and open it for someone with arthritis. Such devices could keep track of a person's medications and issue reminders to take pills on a correct schedule. Senior care facilities in Japan are already using robots in several ways. Robot therapy offers companionship to lonely patients as robotic dogs wander the halls of nursing homes much the same way that real animals are used in nursing homes in the United States. The mechanical AI dogs offer the added benefit of being able to remember the names of an Alzheimer's patient's children.

Researchers at Carnegie Mellon Institute are testing Pearl, a nursebot. Only four feet high with a cute face, Pearl will eventually be able to understand spoken commands, respond to questions, and keep elderly patients on a regular schedule.

A less sophisticated piece of equipment that may come on the market sooner than Pearl is the AI walker. The walker is equipped with sonar detectors to prevent a patient from bumping into objects and a laser range finder and mapping software to figure out where it is going when the person using the walker does not know. It is also able to move itself out of the way when not in use and come when called.

Other nonrobotic assisted cognitive systems combine AI software, global positioning technology, sensor networks, and even infrared identification badges so that patients with early-stage Alzheimer's will be able to use AI personal digital assistants. One new product for patients is a handheld activity compass that is capable of memorizing a person's daily routine. It can offer suggestions when the person becomes confused or provide directions when the person gets lost. The person only needs to click on a picture of the desired destination and a directional arrow appears on the handheld screen and points in the proper direction. If the destination is not clear in the patient's mind, the handheld compass could offer suggestions based on the time of day, daily routine, and current location. For example, the compass could direct a patient who loses his or her way in a doctor's office building toward the proper office or the exit.

An Alzheimer's patient's house could be wired with a network of sensors to become a "smart home." Heat sensors could warn the resident that a hot stove had been left unattended. Motion sensors could detect periods of inactivity and signal an outside agency or call for an ambulance if someone were injured. In twenty years, the baby boomers who now surf the Internet and use e-mail and instant messaging to keep up with friends will be ready for the high-tech elder care that is now being perfected.

But other researchers are looking at ways to assist a failing brain directly with artificial intelligence so that there would be no need for smart homes or nursebots.

They see the future of artificial intelligence as a merging of the best of both biological and mechanical worlds.

Cyborg Science

In the movie *Star Trek: First Contact*, Captain Jean-Luc Picard is captured by a race of creatures called the Borg that are part man and part machine. Picard's human parts are slowly replaced by wire, metal, and silicon. The idea might seem unsettling for a squeamish moviegoer, but it is exciting to AI researchers and neuroscientists who hope to make bionics a reality—to create not a hostile Borg race that would try to take over the universe but artificial cognitive parts that would be available when a person's biological parts fail.

This concept is not so far-fetched. Already there are bionic parts for people who need them. Cochlear implants connect the electronics of a silicon device directly to the nervous system for those who cannot hear. Artificial arms and legs are available for those who have lost a limb, and pacemakers provide the electrical stimulus to regulate a faulty heart. With machinery and computer power, scientists can now make whole what was once broken. If the human body becomes weak, mechanical parts are sturdy and replaceable. But what about a person's brain?

A person's memory can grow dim over the years and holds a finite amount of information. A person's thoughts, ideas, and knowledge are lost after death. But a computer brain can have a limitless amount of memory stored on an infinite number of disks. The knowledge it contains can be downloaded and shared among other computers so that it is never lost. Some AI researchers, like Hans Moravec at the Carnegie Mellon Institute, predict that someday there will be ways to download the contents of the human brain into a computer so that it would "live" forever.

But for now, the future may lie in the arm of one AI researcher, Kevin Warwick of Reading University.

Warwick had a silicon chip implanted in his arm to record the signals that pass through his nerves as he moves. For example, the signals recorded when he wiggles his fingers will be broadcast through a tiny radio antenna to a computer, which will store the signals on a hard drive. Although other researchers have criticized the project as a publicity stunt, Warwick hopes that eventually the computer will be able to play back the signals so that his nervous system will be triggered and wiggle his fingers in response. If these kinds of brain signals are transmittable, it very well could mean that a man could direct a machine's actions by simply thinking about them, and a machine could direct a man's actions.

Why pursue a man and machine mind meld? Some researchers believe that a thinking robot will never be

As part of his AI research, Kevin Warwick had a silicon chip implanted in his arm to monitor the signals his brain transmits to his nerves.

very effective because of the inherent limitations of trying to duplicate biological systems with machinery. But they hope that a mix of biological intelligence, artificial intelligence, and robotics will produce high-level thinking machines and effective replacement parts for people with mental and physical disabilities. The people who could benefit most would be those with paralyzed limbs, but the U.S. Department of Defense's DARPA is also interested in mind-controlled battlebots and airplanes that can be directed by thoughts alone. DARPA funds a Human Assisted Neural Devices Program to find ways to integrate human thought processes into computer operations.

If it seems impossible, think again. The mind meld has begun, although not with the human species. In a lab at Duke University's Center for Neuroengineering, a robotic arm swings from side to side, pivots, and straightens as if to snatch something unseen out of the air. The clamplike hand opens and closes, then shoots out again in a different direction. There is no visible sign of what is controlling the arm except for a trail of tangled cables that snake out the door and down the hall to a small, darkened room.

Inside that room is the power behind the robotic arm—a small monkey strapped in a chair. The monkey is motionless, staring at a computer monitor watching a dot move around the screen. As the monkey watches the dot, its brain is directing the robot arm with its thoughts, which trigger signals picked up by electrodes buried in its brain. The signal is transmitted through the cables to the robotic arm.

Another related research project has created the first robot that moves using the biological neural network that is no longer in a living body. Called the Hybrot, it is a small circular device with movements that are controlled by neural cells taken from the brain of a rat. "We call it the 'Hybrot' because it is a hybrid of living and robotic components," says Steve Potter, a professor at Georgia Institute of Technology. "We hope to learn how

Neurobiologist Miguel Nicolelis has programmed a robotic arm that responds to the brain signals of monkeys.

living neural networks may be applied to the artificial computing systems of tomorrow." Researchers also hope to learn about learning. "Learning is often defined as a lasting change in behavior, resulting from experience,"[26] Potter says, and in order for a being to experience the world, the brain needs a body.

A droplet that contains a few thousand living neurons from a rat's brain is placed on a special petri dish fitted with sixty microelectrodes. This functions as the robot's brain. The cell's activities are recorded by the electrodes and transmitted to the robot's body, a small circular device that can fit in the palm of a hand. The robot's body then moves in response to the electrical impulses received by the cell. The Hybrot is not cyborg material yet, but it is a start.

AI Ethics

The interfacing of brain and machines and robots taking care of grandparents are unsettling ideas to some people. Much time, effort, and technology has been, and will continue to be, spent on making machines that are intelligent. But not as much attention has been paid to a code of ethics to guide the use of artificial intelligence. The Internet has already called into question people's right to privacy and intellectual property rights that protect writers and other creators who show their work online.

In recent years experts have tried to forecast future concerns regarding the ethics of artificial intelligence, particularly about people's perceptions of themselves. Would people become lazy if they had robots to do all the dull, dirty jobs for them? Would people become less caring if they dealt with robots all day long? How would attitudes change if humans were no longer the only humanlike intelligent beings on the planet?

What if scientists are successful in creating truly autonomous AI? Will laws change? This dilemma was played out in an episode of *Star Trek: The Next Generation* when the robot Data had to stand trial to establish his rights to decide his own fate. The prosecution contended that he was no more aware than a toaster. If a creature behaves like a human, should it also enjoy human rights?

So far, science has followed where fiction has led, designing artificial creatures and intelligent machines that used to dwell only in the minds of writers and filmmakers. But what if the ultimate fictional horror story happens? What if machines become so smart that mankind loses control over them? Here too fiction has been first to address this possibility. In his classic novel *I, Robot*, Isaac Asimov wrote the Three Laws of Robotics so that humans would always maintain control. Asimov's fictional robots had superhuman strength and superhuman intelligence, so it was vital to keep that power in check. His three laws stated:

1. A robot may not injure a human being, or, through inaction, allow a human being to come to harm.
2. A robot must obey the orders given to it by human beings except when such would conflict with the First Law.
3. A robot must protect its own existence as long as such protection does not conflict with the First and Second Laws.[27]

Someday hardwiring AI systems with similar safeguards may be necessary if intelligent robots become commonplace or if AI systems are used more often in people's lives. It will need to be addressed so that those who are conducting the research are aware of the power and potential hazards that exist. "In any kind of technology there are risks," says Ron Brackman of DARPA. The branch of the military that funds much of the AI research in the United States does not take the ethical issues for granted. DARPA consults neurologists, psychologists, and philosophers to help sort out the future before it gets here. After all, artificial intelligence systems are used to monitor and track threats from other countries and deploy long-range missiles and other weapons. It is comforting to know that the military takes such ideas seriously. "We're not stumbling down some blind alley," Brackman says. "We're very cognizant of these issues."[28]

The question of whether intelligent machines could take over the world may never come into play. But other, more mundane questions will demand difficult answers. For example, what are the legal responsibilities of artificial intelligence systems that function as

Sony's humanoid robot Qrio and robotic dog Aibo can interact with each other despite the fact that they were designed independently.

decision makers? Banks frequently blame computer error for adding too much interest or withdrawing too much money from accounts, but what would happen if a medical expert system were to fail to diagnose a fatal disease or recommend a procedure that proved deadly to a patient? Who would be responsible—the company that uses the system, the programmers who set it up, or the experts who supplied the information? These and many more questions are already being discussed in boardrooms and labs around the world.

AI Power

Most people do not realize how much of their lives are affected by AI and cannot imagine how it will expand in the years to come. People surf the Internet with AI search engines and encounter intelligent agents when they buy a product from a Web site. Their bank accounts and credit cards are monitored with AI software, and transportation systems run smoothly with artificial intelligence programs. Every e-mail and every cell phone call is routed using AI networks. The appliances in the kitchen and the car in the driveway all have parts that use artificial intelligence technology. And that is only a small taste of what AI has accomplished in the last sixty years.

The future promises many more advances with robotic assistants, microscopic systems, and cyborg technology. "As this enormous computing power is combined with . . . advances of the physical sciences . . . enormous power is being unleashed," says Bill Joy of Microsoft. "These combinations open up the opportunity to completely redesign the world."[29] And, for better or worse, how people choose to use that power is up to them.

Notes

Chapter 1: The First Thinking Machinery

1. Quoted in Neil Gershenfeld, *When Things Start to Think*. New York: Henry Holt, 1999, p. 125.
2. Alan Turing, "Computing Machinery and Intelligence," *Mind*, October 1950. www.loebner.net/Prizef/TuringArticle.html.
3. Gary Kasparov, "The Day That I Sensed a New Kind of Intelligence," *Time*, March 25, 1996, p. 55.
4. Quoted in James M. Pethokoukis, "Robotrading 101," *U.S. News & World Report*, January 28, 2002, p. 23.

Chapter 2: Mind Versus Metal

5. Gershenfeld, *When Things Start to Think*, p. 123.
6. Quoted in David Freedman, *Brainmakers*. New York: Simon & Schuster, 1994, p. 22.
7. Rodney Brooks, *Flesh and Machines*. New York: Pantheon, 2002, p. 46.

Chapter 3: Everyday AI

8. Quoted in Attila Narin, "Myths of Artificial Intelligence," December 1993. www.narin.com.
9. Quoted in Charles Wardell, "The Souped-Up Kitchen," *Popular Science*, March 2004, p. 30.
10. Quoted in Stephen Cass, "Mind Games," *Spectrum Online*, December 2002. www.spectrum.ieee.org.
11. Quoted in Cass, "Mind Games."

Chapter 4: AI and Robotics

12. Quoted in Sean Price, "Robot World," *National Geographic Kids*, January 2003, p. 28.
13. Quoted in Peter Menzel and Faith D'Aluisio, *Robo Sapiens*. Boston: MIT Press, 2000, p. 111.

14. Quoted in National Science Foundation, "Search-and-Rescue Robots Practice Emergency Response to Simulated Earthquakes," 2001. www.sciencedaily.com.

15. Quoted in Ramon Lopez, "Daddy Warbots," *Popular Science*, March 2004, p. 65.

16. Quoted in Jim Wilson, "Tiny Robots Go to War," *Popular Mechanics*, March 2004, p. 13.

Chapter 5: In Pursuit of the Mechanical Man

17. Quoted in Clifton Coles, "Humanoid Robots: Functional and Fun," *Futurist*, January/February 2004, p. 12.

18. Quoted in *Discover*, "The Future of Humanoid Robots," March 2000, p. 84.

19. Quoted in "The Future of Humanoid Robots," p. 84.

20. Quoted in Gershenfeld, *When Things Start to Think*, p. 135.

21. Brooks, *Flesh and Machines*, p. 91.

22. Quoted in Thomas Hayden, "The Age of Robots," *U.S. News & World Report*, April 23, 2001, p. 47.

Chapter 6: The Future of AI

23. Quoted in Chuck Squatriglia, "New Breed of U.S. Spy Is a Tiny Fly," *TechGeek*, June 27, 2002. www.techgeek.com.

24. Quoted in Mark Baard, "AI to Assist Alzheimer's Patients," *Wired News*, 2002. www.wired.com.

25. Quoted in Lori Valigra, "Looking Technology in the Eye," *Christian Science Monitor*, February 5, 2004. www.csmonitor. com.

26. Quoted in Megan McRainey, "Georgia Tech Researchers Use Lab Cultures to Control Robotic Device," Georgia Institute of Technology, 2003. www.gatech.edu.

27. Isaac Asimov, *I, Robot*. New York: Doubleday, 1950, unpaged.

28. Quoted in Kathleen Melymuka, "Good Morning, Dave . . . The Defense Department Is Working on a Self-Aware Computer," *Computerworld*, November 11, 2002, unpaged.

29. Quoted in Alexandra Hanson-Harding, "Smart Machines," *Junior Scholastic*, September 17, 2001, p. 6.

Glossary

algorithm: A step-by-step procedure for solving a specific problem.

artificial neural network (ANN): A computer program created to mimic the structure of the human brain.

autonomous: Able to act independently, without any help or outside instructions.

axon: The part of a neuron that sends nerve impulses away from the nerve cell's body.

binary code: The computer language represented with 1s and 0s.

bit: A unit of computer information.

dendrite: The part of a nerve cell that sends impulses to the cell body.

ethics: A set of values or rules that govern what is good and bad behavior.

expert system: A computer program that has the knowledge and experience of one or more experts in a particular subject, such as stock market trading.

fuzzy logic: A decision-making computer program that can process incomplete or imprecise information in the way that a human brain can.

hardware: The nuts, bolts, and electrical circuits of a computer or robot.

knowledge base: The stored information and rules used by expert systems to solve a problem or make a decision.

neuron: A cell that transmits nerve impulses.

program: The list of instructions that tells a computer what to do.

search engine: A computer program that analyzes information in Internet Web pages for key words.

silicon: The material used in making computer chips.

software: The computer program that instructs the computer or robot.

soma: The body of a nerve cell.

synapse: The gap between two neurons that transmits a nerve impulse.

threshold: The level above which something will happen; used in training a computer.

For Further Reading

Books

Isaac Asimov, *I, Robot*. New York: Doubleday, 1950. An old book but a classic science fiction tale, nevertheless, of humanoid robots taking over the world.

Gareth Branwyn, *Absolute Beginner's Guide to Building Robots*. New York: Pearson Education, 2003. A clearly written how-to book for those who want to design and build robots with easy-to-find materials.

Clive Gifford, *How to Build a Robot*. New York: Franklin Watts, 2001. This book covers the basics of robotics and the mechanics involved.

Ian Graham, *Artificial Intelligence*. Chicago: Heinemann, 2003. An easy-to-read book that looks at robotics and AI research.

Robert L. Perry, *Artificial Intelligence*. New York: Franklin Watts, 2000. The author discusses how artificial intelligence developed and where it is headed in the future.

Alex Woolf, *Artificial Intelligence: The Impact on Our Lives*. Austin, TX: Raintree Steck-Vaughn, 2003. A general overview of AI and its applications.

Web Sites

American Association for Artificial Intelligence (www.aaai.org). A comprehensive site about AI history, theories, and current research, with many links to other sites.

Mars Exploration Rover Mission (http://marsrover.jpl.nasa.gov). Follow the robots Opportunity and Spirit as they explore the surface of Mars.

Massachusetts Institute of Technology Humanoid Robotics Group (www.ai.mit.edu). This site shows how the robots Cog and Kismet work.

Robot Hall of Fame (www.robothalloffame.org). Run by the Carnegie Mellon Institute, this fun site gives students the vital statistics of famous robots such as Sojourner, HAL 9000, and R2-D2.

Works Consulted

Books

Rodney Brooks, *Flesh and Machines*. New York: Pantheon, 2002. A fascinating account of Brooks's research in AI and robotics at MIT.

Daniel Crevier, *AI: The Tumultuous History of the Search for Artificial Intelligence*. New York: BasicBooks, 1993. An in-depth account of the early years of AI and the researchers who pursued it.

David Freedman, *Brainmakers*. New York: Simon & Schuster, 1994. A fascinating look at the research in and debate over AI.

Thomas M. Georges, *Digital Soul*. Boulder, CO: Westview, 2003. A balanced discussion of the possibilities and ethics of AI.

Neil Gershenfeld, *When Things Start to Think*. New York: Henry Holt, 1999. A thought-provoking look at the future of thinking machines.

James Martin, *After the Internet: Alien Intelligence*. Washington, DC: Capital, 2000. This book deals with the possibilities of computer technology and its place in the world.

Peter Menzel and Faith D'Aluisio, *Robo Sapiens*. Boston: MIT Press, 2000. Illustrated by amazing photographs, this book includes interviews with some of the major scientists in AI.

Periodicals

Clifton Coles, "Humanoid Robots: Functional and Fun," *Futurist*, January/February 2004.

Discover, "The Future of Humanoid Robots," March 2000.

Economist, "AI by Another Name," March 2002.

Alexandra Hanson-Harding, "Smart Machines," *Junior Scholastic*, September 17, 2001.

Thomas Hayden, "The Age of Robots," *U.S. News & World Report*, April 23, 2001.

Joseph Hooper, "Clash of the Headless Humvees," *Popular Science*, March 2004.

Steven Johnson, "Smart Robot Pet Tricks," *Discover*, February 2004.

Gary Kasparov, "The Day That I Sensed a New Kind of Intelligence," *Time*, March 25, 1996.

Ramon Lopez, "Daddy Warbots," *Popular Science*, March 2004.

Kathleen Melymuka, "Good Morning, Dave . . . The Defense Department Is Working on a Self-Aware Computer," *Computerworld*, November 11, 2002.

James M. Pethokoukis, "Robotrading 101," *U.S. News & World Report*, January 28, 2002.

Sean Price, "Robot World," *National Geographic Kids*, January 2003.

Mindy Sink, "An Electronic Cop That Plays Hunches," *New York Times*, November 2, 2002.

Brad Stone, "Real World Robots," *Newsweek*, March 24, 2003.

William Underhill, "Hard-Wired for Survival," *Newsweek International*, May 6, 2002.

Charles Wardell, "The Souped-Up Kitchen," *Popular Science*, March 2004.

Peter Weiss, "Electronic Skin Senses Touch," *Science News*, January 17, 2004.

Jim Wilson, "Tiny Robots Go to War," *Popular Mechanics*, March 2004.

Internet Sources

Mark Baard, "AI to Assist Alzheimer's Patients," *Wired News*, 2002. www.wired.com.

Stephen Cass, "Mind Games," *Spectrum Online*, December 2002. www.spectrum.ieee.org.

Cycorp, "Overview of Cycorp's Research and Development," 2001. www.cyc.com.

Tom Harris, "How Robots Work," *How Stuff Works*, 2004. www.howstuffworks.com.

Megan McRainey, "Georgia Tech Researchers Use Lab Cultures to Control Robotic Device," Georgia Institute of Technology, 2003. www.gatech.edu.

Attila Narin, "Myths of Artificial Intelligence," 1993. www.narin.com.

National Science Foundation, "Search-and-Rescue Robots Practice Emergency Response to Simulated Earthquakes," 2001. www.sciencedaily.com.

Chuck Squatriglia, "New Breed of U.S. Spy Is a Tiny Fly," *TechGeek*, 2002. www.techgeek.com.

Richard Stenger, "Eight-Eyed Robot Blasts Off for Mars," CNN.com, June 10, 2003. www.cnn.com.

Bijal P. Trivedi, "Search-and-Rescue Robots Tested at New York Disaster Site," *National Geographic Today*, September 2004. http://news.nationalgeographic.com.

Alan Turing, "Computing Machinery and Intelligence," *Mind*, October 1950. www.loebner.net/Prizef/TuringArticle.html.

Lori Valigra, "Looking Technology in the Eye," *Christian Science Monitor*, February 5, 2004. www.csmonitor.com.

Index

Picture Credits

Cover photo: © Sam Ogden/Photo Researchers, Inc.
Toshiyuki Aizawa/Reuters/Landov, 62, 96
AP/Wide World Photos, 23, 45, 69, 85, 93
© Bettmann/CORBIS, 15, 17
Mike Blake/Reuters/Landov, 66
Rebecca Cook/Reuters/Landov, 55
© CORBIS, 14
© Ralph Crane/Time Life Pictures/Getty Images, 24
Michal Dolezal/EPA/Landov, 72
© Dreamworks/The Kobal Collection, 47
© Extempo Systems, Inc. (www.extempo.com), 50
© Mauro Fermariello/Photo Researchers, Inc. , 39
Getty Images, 42
© James King-Holmes/Photo Researchers, Inc., 91
© LucasFilm/20th Century Fox/The Kobal Collection, 10
© David Mack/Photo Researchers, Inc., 86
Aladin Abdel Naby/Reuters/Landov, 61
NASA/Ames Research Center, 59
NASA/Jet Propulsion Laboratory/Caltech, 58 (both)
Brandy Noon, 19, 31, 34, 46, 73
© Sam Ogden/Photo Researchers, Inc., 70, 76, 80, 81
© David Parker/Photo Researchers, Inc., 53
© Roger Ressmeyer/CORBIS, 29
© Mark Thomas/Photo Researchers, Inc., 83

About the Author

Peggy Thomas is the author of more than ten nonfiction books for children and young adults, as well as numerous magazine and newspaper articles. Several of her books have been placed on the New York Public Library's recommended list of Books for the Teen Age and listed as an NSTA-CBC Outstanding Science Trade Book for Children. She received her master's degree in anthropology from the State University of New York at Buffalo and lives in Middleport, New York, with her husband and two children.